They Did What!?

THE FUNNY, WEIRD, WONDERFUL,
OUTRAGEOUS, AND STUPID THINGS
FAMOUS PEOPLE HAVE DONE

BOB FENSTER

Andrews McMeel
Publishing

Kansas City

02 03 04 05 06 MVP 10 9 8 7 6 5 4 3 2

ISBN: 0-7407-2218-2

Library of Congress Control Number: 2001095898

Book design by Lisa Martin
Illustrations by Matt Taylor

This book is dedicated totally to my wife,

Anne Bothwell,

the most famous person in my life.

There, Anne, are you happy now?

CONTENTS

INTRODUCTION

"Always sit next to a man in a turban," the writer Gore Vidal advised. "You get photographed more."

Famous people wear a lot of turbans. They dress only in white, if they dress at all. They rent yachts for their Pekingese. They name their kids Zowie, God, and Legal Tender.

They are, happily and otherwise, weird, which is one reason we love them so.

I used to write about famous people for a newspaper that wanted only the normal stories. But every time I'd come back to the office from a celebrity interview, one of the editors would ask, "Now tell me the good stuff you can't put in your story."

They didn't mean scandals because that was common enough. They wanted to know about the quirks, the obsessions, the egos of the famous, the odd things celebrities will reveal when you get them off-subject.

Why the editors didn't want me to put these eccentricities into my stories is another story, the one about the dulling of American newspapers and their fawning over stars.

But I saved all the funny, strange tales I picked up along the way (and through my subsequent research) and put them in this book: which genius's wife put the toothpaste on his toothbrush every night, why Gary Cooper paid by check, and the advantages of naked celebrity Ping-Pong.

People become famous for a crazy range of reasons. But what they do with their fame is beautifully strange, often enough to make your jaw drop as you exclaim, "They did what!?"

So let's peep into that exotic, gated world.

PART 1

YOU'VE
GOT TO BE
KIDDING

CHAPTER 1

Punching out the deaf

*Outrageous acts famous people
never get in trouble for*

As the NBA season began, basketball star Derrick Coleman gave his coach a blank check. For playing time? No, to cover the fines for all the team rules he intended to break.

If you were the kind of kid who always got in trouble for pulling wacky stunts, you should become famous because celebrities can do the weirdest things and get away with them.

~~~

When American actress Tallulah Bankhead moved to London, she bought a car but couldn't figure out how to get around town. So whenever she went anywhere, she hired a taxi to drive in front and lead her to her destination.

~~~

When Bob Dylan gave up being a folk singer and played his first set with a rock band, folk purist Pete Seeger (an avowed pacifist) tried to shut down Dylan's show by cutting the power cable with an ax.

Kid McCoy became the welterweight champ in 1896. Earlier in his career, he had shown what it took to survive in the ring when he fought a boxer who was completely deaf.

By the third round, McCoy had figured out that his opponent couldn't hear the bell. So he stepped back and motioned to the other fighter that the bell had rung to end the round (it hadn't).

As the other boxer dropped his hands and turned to his corner, McCoy jumped in and knocked him out.

~~~

Ernst August, prince of Hanover and husband to Princess Caroline of Monaco, was caught in a photo urinating on the fence of the Turkish pavilion at Expo 2000, the world fair that the German city hoped would promote Hanover as a tourist attraction.

~~~

When movie director John Ford fell a day behind in the shooting schedule on one of his pictures, studio boss Sam Goldwyn complained about the cost of the delay.

Goldwyn argued that Ford should speed up production and shoot five pages of script a day. So Ford ripped out five pages from the script and handed them to his boss. "There," he said, "now we're back on schedule."

Eccentric baseball pitcher Rube Waddell was once at bat when the catcher threw to second base to pick off a runner. The throw sailed wide into the outfield, and the runner took off, rounded third, and headed home.

As the throw came in for a play at the plate, Waddell stepped up and swung at it, knocking the ball over the fence. Not a home run, of course, interference and an out.

Why'd he do it? Waddell explained that it was the first pitch he'd seen all day that he could hit.

Frederick II, eighteenth-century king of Prussia, held an official inspection of the Berlin prison, where all the prisoners took advantage of his presence to plead their innocence.

All except one man, who readily admitted that he was guilty of robbery and deserved his punishment.

The king ordered this man's immediate release. "I will not have him kept in this prison," Frederick explained, "where he will corrupt all the fine innocent people who occupy it."

Psychedelic rocker Grace Slick of Jefferson Airplane, performed topless in the rain because she didn't want to ruin her silk blouse.

Later, she threatened to spike President Nixon's tea with LSD. We're pretty sure she didn't, although Watergate may make you think otherwise.

SO OUTRAGEOUS YOU HAVE TO ADMIRE THEM

1. According to political columnist Jack Germond, Averell Harriman, governor of New York in the 1950s and an unsuccessful candidate for president, "wore a hearing aid but turned it on only when he was talking."

When other people had something to say, the gov turned it back off.

2. When English officials told Elizabeth Taylor that she could not enter the country unless she put her four Pekingese into quarantine, the movie star rented a yacht for $2,500 a week and anchored it offshore as a floating kennel.

3. If you're a prince, it's considered normal: Eighteenth-century Austrian Prince Wenzel von Kaunitz-Rietburg changed his clothes at least thirty times a day.

But the world title for Clothes King goes not to a Hollywood superstar but to King Augustus III of Poland, who had so many clothes they filled two entire halls of his eighteenth-century palace.

Each outfit came with its own wig, cane, and sword. Servants kept consultation books containing charts of all of his clothes for proper rotational dressing schedules.

How absentminded are famous people? Meryl Streep left her just-claimed Oscar for *Kramer vs. Kramer* on the back of a toilet during the 1979 Academy Awards show.

Catherine the Great, empress of Russia, locked her hairdresser in prison. For a bad haircut? No, a good one. The empress didn't want the hairdresser styling anyone else.

Colonel Robert McCormick, right-wing publisher of the *Chicago Tribune* in the 1930s, was labeled the "greatest mind of the fourteenth century."

McCormick's front-page headline describing the 1936 Democratic National Convention: SOVIETS MEET AT PHILADELPHIA.

The great Greek orator Demosthenes (famous for curing his stammer by speaking with a mouth full of pebbles) once dug a room underground so he could practice his oratory in private.

To avoid the temptation to leave the room in search of company, Demosthenes shaved off half his hair so he would be too embarrassed to show himself in public.

While Mia Farrow was filming the difficult horror movie *Rosemary's Baby*, husband Frank Sinatra sent her something on the set: not a gift—divorce papers.

Clark Gable did not want to star with Jeanette MacDonald in the movie *San Francisco,* but he was forced into it by the studio bosses. To get his revenge, Gable ate something before their first screen kiss: garlic.

~~~

Why would a playwright boo his own play?

Charles Lamb was a successful literary critic in the 1800s but a failure in the theater. When one of his plays was roundly booed on opening night, Lamb joined in the jeers, explaining later that he did so because he was "afraid of being mistaken for the author."

~~~

Before Henry David Thoreau became a famous writer extolling the virtues of the natural life, he worked as a schoolteacher. When he was reprimanded by the head of the school for being too easy on students who misbehaved, Thoreau chose six students at random and caned them. Then he quit.

~~~

New York Times theater critic Alexander Woollcott was so abusive in cutting up plays and actors in his reviews that the Shubert brothers banned him from all their theaters.

Publicity from the resulting lawsuit did wonders for Woollcott's notoriety and career. "They threw me out; now I'm basking in the fierce white light that beats upon the thrown," he crowed.

The producers recouped the publicity by inviting the savage critic back into their theaters, thus triumphantly capping a controversy that paid dividends to both sides.

TEMPER TANTRUMS
OF THE FAMOUS

1. In the 2000 Samsung Open in England, tennis star Goran Ivanisevic smashed three tennis rackets because he was having a tough match. Then he realized he had no more rackets left.

With nothing left to smash or hit a tennis ball, Ivanisevic had to forfeit the tourney.

2. When Olympic bad girl Tonya Harding turned figure skating into a full-contact sport, she needed a boyfriend to club her rival in the knee.

But she learned her lesson, and when it came time to smash her next boyfriend in the nose with a hubcap, she did the job herself.

Harding later went into therapy and reunited with her battered man. Anyone taking bets on how long that relationship lasts?

3. The sporting world was shocked when hockey player Donald Brashear was viciously assaulted on the ice by opposing player Marty McSorley in 1999. McSorley was convicted of assault with a deadly weapon (his hockey stick).

A year later the victim, Brashear, was charged with assaulting a man who asked the hockey player's wife to take her baby out of a gym. The sporting world was no longer shocked.

4. John Sebastian, lead singer of the mellow band The Lovin' Spoonful, grew so sick of fan adulation that during one show he swung his guitar at girls who were pressed up against the stage.

Charles Hamilton, a wealthy eighteenth-century British eccentric, hired a hermit to live in the garden of his estate, providing his new employee with a man-made cave, a hair shirt, and a Bible.

~~~

Writer and wit Marc Connelly once enlivened a dull society party by introducing himself as the editor of *Popular Wading,* "the magazine of shallow-water sports."

~~~

President Herbert Hoover came up with a clever way to get boring after-dinner speakers to sit down: He'd pass over a note telling the droner, "Your fly is open."

~~~

When actor Fred Astaire bought some racing horses, he sneaked out in the middle of the night and painted his racing colors on the mailboxes of mansions all over Beverly Hills.

~~~

If only all Hollywood stars were this honest. Ava Gardner (in a restaurant after cocktails): "People think I'm the type who would take the busboy out back. Well, I just might."

~~~

Jerry Lee Lewis and Elvis Presley once rode their motorcycles naked through the streets of Nashville.

~~~

French film star Brigitte Bardot: "I have always adored beautiful young men. Just because I grow older, my taste doesn't change. So if I can still have them, why not?"

IN THE ANGELINA JOLIE WANTS A DEPARTMENT TO HERSELF DEPARTMENT

1. The movie star has a tattoo on her left forearm of a quote from Tennessee Williams: "A prayer for the wild at heart, kept in cages," which she got with her mother in attendance.

2. Her other tattoos include the Japanese sign for death, two American Indian symbols, a dragon, and a large cross.

3. Angelina married actor Jonny Lee Miller wearing a unique bridal gown: black leather pants and a white shirt, on which she wrote her husband's name in her own blood.

4. When Angelina married actor Billy Bob Thornton, they each wore vials of the other's blood.

5. How does Angelina Jolie explain the wilder side of her nature? "You're young, you're drunk, you're in bed, you have knives; shit happens."

CHAPTER 2

Elvis, you mind moving that truck?

Early failure among the famous

We've all been rejected, and some of us learn to take no for an answer. That's how they narrow down the field.

Not the famous. They all said no to no.

~~~

It took Beat poet Jack Kerouac only three weeks to write the rambling novel *On the Road,* which eventually became the bible of a restless generation. Took him six years to find someone who would publish the book.

~~~

In 1954, Elvis Presley was kicked out of the Grand Ole Opry with the recommendation that he go back to driving a truck.

In 1955, Elvis auditioned for a spot on Arthur Godfrey's *Talent Scouts* and was turned down.

~~~

When Burt Bacharach was trying to break into song-writing, he went through a solid year of rejections. "They'd stop you after eight bars," he recalled. "Connie Francis lifted the needle off the demo."

Henry David Thoreau became famous for writing *Walden*. But his earlier book, *A Week on the Concord and Merrimack Rivers,* was a complete bust, selling fewer than three hundred copies out of a first printing of one thousand.

Thoreau bought the remaining copies of the book himself and wrote in his journal, "I now have a library of nearly nine hundred volumes, over seven hundred of which I wrote myself."

Teachers at John Murray Anderson's Dramatic School in New York sent a young student home because she was "too shy" to make an actress out of her.

The girl's name? Lucille Ball.

As a recluse and an unknown writer, Emily Dickinson showed some of her poetry to the literary lion Thomas Wentworth Higginson, who advised her not to try to publish her poems because they were "strange" and "peculiar."

Dickinson, after her death, was recognized as one of the world's great poets. Higginson is no longer recognizable.

In George Washington's first action as a military leader, he led a small contingent of colonial militiamen against the French in the Ohio River Valley, was captured, and was sent back to Virginia. A year later, he returned as aide to a British general and again was defeated by the French.

He eventually had better luck fighting against the British than he did fighting for them.

The Jimi Hendrix Experience once opened for the Monkees. They were booed by fans and thrown off the tour, Jimi and the Experience that is.

~~~

When Percy Bysshe Shelley's early poetry was rejected by England's publishers, he paid to have the poems printed, then sealed them inside bottles and cast them out to sea.

His subsequent poems had better distribution, as he became one of the greatest romantic poets ever.

~~~

It took Jane Austen seventeen years to find a publisher for *Pride and Prejudice*.

WHAT DO THESE FAMOUS PEOPLE HAVE IN COMMON?

Inventor Thomas Edison; writers Mark Twain, Charles Dickens, Noël Coward, and Sean O'Casey; and ex-Beatle Ringo Starr?

They didn't finish grade school.

Levi Strauss was a flop as a tentmaker in the California gold fields of 1850. Stuck with bales of denim, he invented blue jeans and sold them for $13.50—a dozen.

Genghis Khan, who became a world conqueror, started in misery and slavery when his father was killed in a tribal dispute and his family was sent into exile.

Then the boy, only nine years old, was abducted by another tribe that yoked him with a wooden collar. Still, he managed to escape and return to his tribe. As a teenager, the Khan led them to conquer an empire that spanned from eastern Europe to China.

~~~

When Leon Bean went into business in 1912, he manufactured a single item: rubber hunting boots. When the boots came apart at the seams, Bean had a stroke of business genius: unconditional returns. The rest is L. L. Bean history.

~~~

When the Everly Brothers tried to break into the music biz, they were turned down by a dozen record labels over two years. When someone finally took a chance on them, they sold millions.

~~~

In 1931, Philadelphian Charles Darrow invented the get-rich game of Monopoly. He was unemployed at the time.

Games manufacturer Parker Bros. rejected Darrow's idea because the game was too complex. Three years later, the company reversed its decision and manufactured Monopoly, which became the best-selling board game of all time.

THE KID'LL NEVER MAKE IT

Slow starters who became famous after seemingly having nothing going for them:

1. In his home town of Ulm, Germany, the young Albert Einstein was regarded as "slow, perhaps retarded" by his schoolteachers. Later on, he did okay for himself, relatively speaking.

2. Michael Faraday was born into poverty in the eighteenth century, had no formal education, and was considered to possess a bad memory.

Faraday went on to become one of history's greatest scientists, discovering the principles of electromagnetic induction, the electric motor, the dynamo, and electrolysis while also discovering stainless steel, benzene, and butylene.

3. George Bernard Shaw, whose plays rank among the world's greatest, earned a total of $20 during his first nine years as a writer.

4. As a teenager, British leader Winston Churchill failed the entrance exams to the Royal Military Academy—twice. (He made it on the third try, and the rest is history.)

5. The great French writer Honoré de Balzac spent ten years as a failure before he had a successful book.

6. Frederick the Great of Prussia was anything but great as a youth. His father, King Frederick, abused the boy, labeling him a weakling. At the age of twenty, Frederick deserted from his father's army, was caught, and was thrown into prison.

Once released, he became the greatest military leader of a war-mad eighteenth century and, surprisingly, a great leader, granting his people more liberties than any other monarch of his time.

Ambrose Burnside, whose style of facial hair gave us side-burns, was a remarkable failure. He graduated near the bottom of his class from West Point, and his munitions work was a financial failure, even though the carbine he developed there was popular.

During the Civil War, he commanded Union troops into one debacle after another, including his attack on Fredericksburg, in which one hundred thousand of his soldiers were slaughtered.

On his wedding day, his bride-to-be was asked if she took this man to be her husband and replied "No" quite sensibly, if belatedly.

~~~

Audie Murphy was turned down by the marines for being too short at five-foot-five. The army took him, and Murphy became one of the greatest fighting heroes of World War II.

~~~

Otto von Bismarck first entered the Prussian civil service but had to resign in debt, then quit a second time after more failure, declaring, "I have never been able to put up with superiors."

Fortunately, he then found a field in which he had no superiors; he became the first chancellor of the German empire.

CHAPTER 3

Stop polishing that coffin and get yourself to Hollywood

The early years of famous people

Before singer Dean Martin became a famous member of Frank Sinatra's Rat Pack, he was a professional boxer, fighting under the name of Kid Crochet (his real name was Dino Crocetti). Martin summed up his fight career this way: "I won all but eleven of twelve fights."

All famous people had to start somewhere. Here's where:

Richard King was a stowaway, a deckhand, and finally a riverboat pilot in the 1830s. When he landed in Texas, he was ignorant of all ranching skills.

Yet the sailor became the most successful cowboy in the Old West, eventually owning a ranch of 1.25 million acres.

Actor-hunk Brad Pitt's first acting job: He played a chicken, wearing a chicken suit to attract customers to El Pollo Loco restaurant.

Titanic director James Cameron got his big break while working as an assistant doing pickup shots for an obscure B-movie called *Galaxy of Terror*.

As a second unit director, Cameron was shooting close-ups of a fake dismembered arm that was supposed to be teeming with maggots. He used mealworms as stunt maggots.

In order to make the worms wriggle, Cameron hooked up a power cord to the arm. An assistant behind the scenes would plug in the cord when the film was rolling.

Two producers were passing through the set when Cameron yelled, "Action!" and the worms writhed on cue.

When he yelled, "Cut!" the worms stopped.

The producers were so amazed at his directorial prowess that they signed him for bigger projects.

~~~

Fame toys with time, demanding years of obscurity, then opening up for fleeting seconds of opportunity.

Take the Wright brothers, who won fame for inventing the first airplane to stay aloft.

They were able to keep their first successful flight in the air for only twelve seconds.

But it took them thirteen years of testing their theories of flight with kite and glider experiments on Kill Devil hill in Kitty Hawk, North Carolina, before they had those successful twelve seconds.

At any time during those thirteen years, other inventors working on flight (and there were plenty who were denied their twelve seconds of fame) could have beaten them into the history books.

WHAT DO THESE FAMOUS PEOPLE HAVE IN COMMON?

American patriots Betsy Ross and Paul Revere, political powers J. Edgar Hoover and Lorenzo de Medici, football player Doak Walker, writer Ouida, Pope Gregory XIII, and Alexander VI?

They were all born on January 1.

When he was considered only an eccentric and not one of America's greatest poets, Walt Whitman would walk the streets of Camden, New Jersey, selling copies of his book *Leaves of Grass* from a pack on his back.

When Little Richard was just starting out in rock 'n' roll, he would hide in the balcony when the master of ceremonies announced his act. Then the spotlight would search the stage, and Little Richard would leap into the light from the balcony, landing in a split.

When Bob Dylan first started to record in the '60s, he'd often write the song a day before a recording session. "All those early songs were first drafts that I never even sang other than when I began to record," he said.

Voted most unlikely to become famous: Young Thomas Edison.

Because his teachers considered Thomas "addled," he was home-schooled by his mother.

The first invention of the boy scientist: feeding a young friend a large dose of gas-producing powder to see if the gas would make the boy float off the ground.

Later, young Edison got a job selling candy on trains and built a lab for himself in a baggage car. He received his first patent when he was twenty-two. He eventually won 1,093 of them.

~~~~~

After the Civil War, Washington Duke came home to Durham with only fifty cents and two blind mules. He went to work growing tobacco and became a millionaire, then left $40 million to start Duke University.

~~~~~

Actor Chris O'Donnell (who played Robin in two *Batman* movies) had an early brush with fame. As a model before he broke into the movies, O'Donnell played a McDonald's counter man who was happy to serve breakfast to superstar Michael Jordan.

BLIND LUCK

1. Vernors, created in Detroit, was the first soda pop made in the United States—and by an accident of war.

In 1862, pharmacist James Vernor was trying to create a new beverage when he was called away to serve in the Civil War. When he returned four years later, the drink he had stored in an oak cask had acquired a delicious gingery flavor. The rest is pop culture history.

2. Actress Holly Hunter got her big break when she met playwright Beth Henley in a stalled elevator. Hunter talked herself into roles in a number of Henley's plays, including *Crimes of the Heart* and *The Miss Firecracker Contest*.

3. Football great Bronko Nagurski, one of the all-time strongest running backs, was discovered in the 1920s when a football scout saw the boy plowing a field on his family farm and stopped to ask directions to another farm (where he'd been told there was a strong kid who could play football).

To give the scout directions, Bronko lifted up the plow and pointed down the road with it. The scout never went down the road. He signed the boy who could lift a plow. Great player, smart scout.

4. Actress Pamela Anderson was sitting in the stands watching a Canadian Football League game when a roving camera scanning spectators settled on her. A producer was watching the shot, and she was discovered.

As a choreographer, Busby Berkeley revolutionized the movie musical in the 1930s. He got his early training in the U.S. Army when he served as an artillery officer who also directed parades.

Although no choreographer staged more elaborate production numbers, involving scores of dancers, Busby Berkeley never took a dancing lesson and was afraid people would laugh at him if they found out.

In 1855, G. F. Swift bought a single steer with $25 he borrowed from his father. He sold the meat for a $10 profit and reinvested.

Within a few years he controlled a million-dollar meat-packing business in Chicago.

Robert Englund, who played the macabre Freddy Krueger of the *Nightmare on Elm Street* movies, got his start in the musical *Godspell* as Judas.

From Judas to Freddy Krueger—interesting transition.

Alan Alda did not sign to play Hawkeye Pierce on the TV show *M*A*S*H* until six hours before filming began on the pilot episode. Without that role, who ever would have heard of Alan Alda?

WHAT FAMOUS PEOPLE DID BEFORE THEY HIT IT BIG

1. Singers
- Sting was a teacher.
- Joe Cocker was a plumber.
- Bo Diddley was a construction worker.
- Chuck Berry was a hairdresser.
- Van Morrison was a window cleaner.
- Elvis Costello was a computer technician.

2. Actors
- Warren Beatty played piano in a cocktail lounge.
- Gene Hackman sold ladies' shoes.
- Danny DeVito was a hairdresser.
- Steve Martin sold Mousketeer ears at Disneyland.
- Pee-wee Herman was a brush salesman.
- Dorothy Lamour ran an elevator in a department store.
- So did Marlon Brando.
- Gregory Peck was a carnival barker.
- Sean Connery polished coffins.
- Also working in the funeral business: comic Whoopi Goldberg, singer Rod Stewart, and actress Angelina Jolie.
- Virginia Madsen sang telegrams inside a gorilla suit, "even though I can't sing a note," she said.

CHAPTER 4

The razor blade on the computer

Unusual inspirations that led to greatness

How is inspiration that leads to fame different from the inspiration that leads to dead ends? Let's find out.

By the nature of their jobs, drama teachers are full of advice. If they weren't, who would study with them? Here's some advice from an unusual drama coach to a struggling young actor: "Don't just do something, stand there."

Which actor took that advice to heart and became a famous movie star? Gary Cooper.

John Montagu, earl of Sandwich, invented the sandwich in 1762 when he got hungry but didn't want to leave the table during a forty-eight-hour poker match.

Elvis: "I wanted to be a singer because I didn't want to sweat."

Although he didn't write many of the Beatles' famous songs, Ringo Starr proved to be a major inspiration for the songs by McCartney and Lennon.

Paul reported: "Ringo would say to us, 'God, it's been a hard day's night.'

"We'd say, 'Say that again.' Ringo talked in titles."

McCartney was also inspired by one of their chauffeurs, who talked about how hard he'd been working. "I've been working eight days a week," the driver explained.

~~~~~

The song "Swinging on a Star" became a huge hit after Bing Crosby sang it in the movie *Going My Way*.

Composer Jimmy Van Heusen found the inspiration for the song from Crosby himself, when he overheard the crooner scold one of his sons: "What do you want to be, a mule?"

~~~~~

How did author L. Frank Baum come up with the name "Oz" for the wizardly wonderland that entranced Dorothy and the rest of us?

He took the name from the label on a filing cabinet: O–Z.

~~~~~

English sprinter Forrest Smithson won a gold medal in the hurdles at the 1908 Olympics while carrying a Bible in his hand during the race.

~~~~~

Mel Brooks's great comedy *The Producers* inspired the title of U2's album *Achtung Baby*.

REVERSE INSPIRATION

Inspiration doesn't always have to be positive and supportive. Sometimes the negative can be just as motivational.

1. While editing his biggest movie, *Titanic*, director James Cameron taped a razor blade to the side of the editing computer with instructions written underneath: "Use only if film sucks!"

2. While struggling to make a living during his early years as a writer, Sherwood Anderson ran into a sympathetic book publisher, who sent him a check each week so that he could concentrate on his manuscripts.

After several weeks, Anderson returned the checks uncashed, explaining, "I find it impossible to work with security staring me in the face."

3. Cher on her childhood: "I was a shy, ugly kid who led a big fantasy life."

4. Lee Marvin says he learned to act in the marines, trying to act unafraid during combat, which brought him a Purple Heart during the bloody invasion of Saipan.

5. Alfred Nobel, whose annual prizes reward the best of human accomplishments, including those in the field of international peace, made his fortune by inventing dynamite, which he developed to save lives after his brother was killed experimenting with another unstable explosive.

The inspiration for the G. I. Joe action figure? John Wayne? Audie Murphy? General MacArthur?

Good guesses, but wrong thinking. G. I. Joe was inspired by Barbie, of course. G. I. Joe was simply a toy manufacturer's attempt to get boys to play with dolls, thereby doubling the Barbie market.

Why aren't dolls action figures? They move just as much as boys' toys.

Steven Spielberg's *E.T.* and *Raiders of the Lost Ark* have inspired countless fantasies among movie lovers. But what inspires Spielberg?

"Before I go off and direct a movie, I always look at four films," he said. "They tend to be *Seven Samurai, Lawrence of Arabia, It's a Wonderful Life,* and *The Searchers.*"

Boris Karloff's portrayal of Frankenstein's monster was the inspiration for the first comic-book illustrations of the Incredible Hulk.

Clark Gable's comic performance in *It Happened One Night* was the inspiration for the cartoon character Bugs Bunny.

R & B singer Tina Turner developed her powerful voice as a child in a farm town where no one had a phone, so they used to shout to each other from house to house.

VISIONS OF FAME

Saints may have visions, but so do famous people, although they tend to see things differently.

1. Pop star Billy Joel dreamed many of his songs, hearing both lyrics and music within dreams, then writing them down upon awakening.

2. German composer Robert Schumann said that his musical ideas were dictated to him by angels. But he also suffered from sound hallucinations and spent the last two years of his life in a mental institution.

3. In 1973, soul singer Al Green was performing in a concert, singing R & B love songs, when he felt the spirit of the Lord call to him. So he gave up soul music and took up preaching and singing with the choir. "I couldn't sing 'Baby, baby' any more," he explained.

4. Florence Nightingale heard the voice of God call her to service at the age of seventeen. But her wealthy parents objected to her becoming a nurse, which was considered a disreputable profession in the 1800s.

Florence persevered. When she and her corps of nurses tended to the British army during the Crimean War, they revolutionized the medical care of soldiers.

5. Singer Frankie Valli was hypnotized as a kid when he saw Frank Sinatra sing at the Paramount in New York. "Someday I'm going to be up there too," he said.

Valli made it just in time, playing the Paramount years later, just before it was torn down.

CHAPTER 5

Mr. Kiss Kiss Bang Bang

The name game

Bart Simpson: "So what's it like to be famous?"

Homer Simpson: "People know your name, but you don't know theirs."

Here we learn some interesting tales about the names behind the big names.

~~~

Gary Cooper's name was actually Frank Cooper. His agent didn't like the sound of Frank, so she changed it to honor her hometown: Gary, Indiana.

Cooper said, "It's a good thing she didn't come from Poughkeepsie."

~~~

When Dustin Hoffman was filming *Tootsie,* the movie was going to be called *Would I Lie to You?*

Hoffman wanted a title change and suggested *Tootsie* because that's what his mother called him when he was a kid.

THE RICH AND FAMOUS ARE JUST LIKE YOU AND ME, EXCEPT WHEN IT COMES TO NAMING THEIR KIDS

1. The Rolling Stones' Keith Richards named his daughter Dandelion.

2. Comic Richard Pryor named his daughter Rain.

3. Jefferson Airplane singer Grace Slick named her daughter God.

4. Actress Barbara Hershey named her son Free.

5. Singer David Bowie named his son Zowie.

6. Actor Sylvester Stallone named his son Sage Moonblood.

7. Jacob Coxey, whose Coxey's Army of the Poor marched to the White House to demand jobs, was so caught up in economic theorizing that he named one of his sons Legal Tender.

8. Football star Warren Sapp, who owns four Mercedes, named his daughter Mercedes. Good thing he doesn't drive Isuzus.

9. Bruce Willis and Demi Moore had three daughters: Rumer Glenn, Scout Larue, and Tallulah Belle.

10. John Wayne named his third son John Ethan. What's so unusual about that? Ethan is the name of the character Wayne played in the western *The Searchers*.

You'd think 007 would be known as Bond, James Bond, all over the world. But when the Bond fad started in the 1960s, he was called something else in Italy: Mr. Kiss Kiss Bang Bang.

~~~~

Tonto became famous for calling the Lone Ranger "Kemo Sabe," which on the radio and TV show meant: "faithful friend."

But in Apache, kemo sabe meant "white shirt," and in Navajo "soggy shrub."

~~~~

Diane Keaton's real name: Diane Hall. The character that won her the Oscar: Annie Hall.

~~~~

Actor Michael Keaton was born Michael Douglas, really, but couldn't use that name in Hollywood because there already was someone using it, the famous Michael Douglas.

So he chose Keaton because he liked Diane Keaton's name, although her real name was Diane Hall.

~~~~

My personal favorite how-a-band-got-its-name story: No one in the blues band Ten Years After could think up a good name until one of them was reading a newspaper story that began: "Ten years after the Russian Revolution . . ."

~~~~

Singer Chubby Checker was named by Dick Clark's wife when she found him imitating Fats Domino.

ORIGINAL NAMES OF NOW FAMOUS PEOPLE

1. Movie star Demi Moore: Demetria Guynes
2. Movie star Meg Ryan: Margaret Hyra
3. Actress Susan Sarandon: Susan Tomaling
4. Singer Sting: Gordon Sumner
5. Singer Shania Twain: Eileen Twain
6. Singer Eddie Money: Eddie Mahoney
7. Singer Seal: Sealhenry Samuel
8. Comedian Sinbad: David Adkins
9. Actor Christian Slater: Christian Hawkins

Country Joe and the Fish, the '60s antiwar band, took their name from a quote by Chairman Mao about how revolutions move through a country like fish.

They wanted to add the folksy "Country Joe" name to the Fish, so Joe McDonald became Country Joe (and the only famous member of the group) because he was the only guy in the band named Joe.

As a kid, Robert De Niro was nicknamed Bobby Milk because of his milky white skin.

Comic actor W. C. Fields used pseudonyms in his movies, particularly for scriptwriting credits. Among his many were Charles Bogle, Otis Criblecoblis, and Mahatma Kane Jeeves.

~~~

When he was starting out in movies, Harrison Ford was billed as Harrison J. Ford so he wouldn't be confused with silent-screen actor Harrison Ford II.

What's the J. stand for? Nothing. The star who stayed famous actually has no middle name.

GREAT NICKNAMES

Think nicknames, think sports. I'll go with baseball, where you'll find:
1. Le Grand Orange (Rusty Staub)
2. The Mahatma (Branch Rickey)
3. The Toy Cannon (Jim Wynn)
4. The Macaroni Pony (Bob Coluccio)
5. The Spaceman (Bill Lee)
6. The Singer Throwing Machine (Bill Singer)
7. The Kitten (Felix Millan)
8. Vinegar Bend (Wilmer Mizell)
9. Death to Flying Things (Bob Ferguson)

Nicolas Cage (who is a Coppola) took his stage name from comic book character Luke Cage.

~~~

Soul singer Barry White: "A lot of babies have been named Barry. If there was a Barry boom in '74, I was the one responsible for it."

~~~

The great Civil War general Ulysses S. Grant wasn't Ulysses S. Grant.

He was Hiram Ulysses Grant but felt humiliated by the initials: HUG. So he switched his names around to Ulysses Hiram Grant.

Then when he was nominated for West Point, the congressman who wrote the recommendation got his name further wrong, writing it as Ulysses Simpson Grant. The young cadet liked those initials, and so did the Union in years to come.

~~~

When actor Walter Matthau singed up for Social Security in 1937, he listed Foghorn as his middle name. (It's not. Do you know anyone whose parents named him Foghorn?)

Matthau feuded with costar Barbra Streisand while filming *Hello, Dolly!* Their mutual dislike spilled over into nicknames. He called her Miss Ptomaine. She called him Old Sewermouth.

When Florence Nightingale Graham opened her first cosmetics shop in Manhattan, she changed her name to Elizabeth Arden (and sent herself a letter addressed: "Dear Elizabeth Arden, good luck.").

~~~

When Ramón Estevez moved to New York City, he couldn't find a place to live. So the would-be actor changed his name, taking the first name Martin from a newspaper story and the second name from Bishop Sheen, "the first TV evangelist. He was also a great actor," movie and TV star Martin Sheen said.

~~~

Cybill Shepherd was named after both her grandfather Cy and her father Bill.

~~~

Comic and filmmaker Albert Brooks decided for some reason not to enter show business under his real name: Albert Einstein.

~~~

Before he became a movie star in America, Jackie Chan was known in his Hong Kong movies by two other names: Chan Kong Sung (which means "born in Hong Kong") and Sing Lung (meaning "already a dragon").

~~~

Soul singer and actress Erykah Badu *(Cider House Rules)* was born with the name Erica Wright. Is Badu an African name? Nope, she made up the word herself, using it to sing scat. Liked the sound of it so much, she made it her name.

NAMED AFTER

1. Actress Shirley MacLaine was named for actress Shirley Temple.

2. Movie star Richard Burton took his professional name from his former schoolmaster, Philip Burton.

3. Movie star Halle Berry was named after the grand old Halle Building in Cleveland, which originally housed the Halle Brothers department store.

4. Actor Michael Caine was born Maurice Micklewhite. The English star took his stage name from the movie *The Caine Mutiny*.

What would his career have been like if he'd been named after the other famous mutiny movie: Michael Bounty.

Horror director John Carpenter reused character names from classic movies. He took the name John T. Chance from John Wayne's character in *Rio Bravo* and gave it to Donald Pleasence's character in *Halloween*.

~~~

Shaka, the African leader who created the Zulu nation in the 1800s, was of lowly birth. His name translates as "intestinal parasite."

Carole Lombard was listed in the credits of an early movie, *Safety in Numbers,* as Carole (instead of Carol as in her previous films).

Studio bosses decided that the extra *e* would now be the official spelling of her name, so she legally changed her name to Carole Lombard.

~~~

Colin Campbell, the nineteenth-century British military leader who gave Britain control of India, was known to his men as "Sir Crawling Camel" for his slow, methodical military maneuvers.

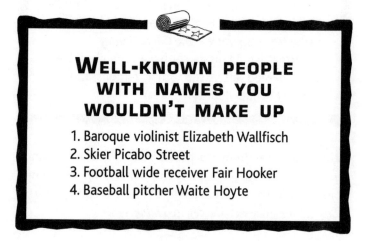

WELL-KNOWN PEOPLE WITH NAMES YOU WOULDN'T MAKE UP

1. Baroque violinist Elizabeth Wallfisch
2. Skier Picabo Street
3. Football wide receiver Fair Hooker
4. Baseball pitcher Waite Hoyte

CHAPTER 6

Oh my God, Garth Brooks is melting

Strange tributes to the famous

When actress Sarah Bernhardt was forced to have a leg amputated in 1915, the manager of the Pan-American Exposition offered her $100,000 for the rights to put the leg on exhibition.

No celebrities reach the peak of fame until some nut pays bizarre tribute to them.

~~~

In 1994, an artist at the Iowa State Fair used 250 pounds of butter to create a life-size statue of country singer Garth Brooks.

~~~

Although Captain James T. Kirk hasn't been born yet, when he is born he'll be born in Riverside, Iowa.

An episode of TV's *Star Trek* said the Enterprise commander was born in a small town in Iowa, so Riverside decided that in the future the fictional character will be born in their small Iowa town.

When Bill Clinton became president, a Chicago baker made a 2,000-pound inaugural cheesecake. The ten layers of solid calories had to be hoisted on top of each other using a forklift.

No report on whether Clinton ate the entire cheesecake himself or shared.

Famed outlaw Jesse James once robbed the bank in Liberty, Kansas. That bank is now the Jesse James Bank Museum.

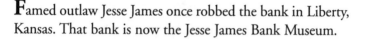

CAPITALISM GONE AMOK

1. After Panamanian strongman Manuel Noriega was arrested in 1990, more than twelve thousand people bet his prisoner number in the state lottery. They all lost.

2. When slugger Mark McGwire shattered the all-time homer mark with seventy in the 1998 season, an infatuated fan produced fake money, a $70 bill with McGwire's picture on the front.

McGwire had to sue the fan to get him to stop making the bills.

3. The Minnesota Timberwolves offered fans free coupons to obtain a bobble-head doll modeled after basketball star Wally Szczerbiak. Three dozen fans used counterfeit coupons to obtain the free dolls illegally.

Most honored among movie actresses? The "Screen's Bad Girl" Mae West, whose name was used for numerous common objects, including a tank, a parachute, a sail, and a cruller.

~~~

Oscar Pierce was a wealthy Texas pioneer. He's famous not for his own accomplishments but because in 1931 the woman who worked as librarian at the Academy of Motion Pictures mentioned that the statue they gave out at the Academy Awards reminded her of her Uncle Oscar. The name stuck.

~~~

When Napoleon was sent into exile, he kissed a flag while saying good-bye to his troops. Loyal French soldiers then burned the flag their general had kissed and ate the ashes.

~~~

After movie idol James Dean was killed in a car crash, fans paid 50 cents each to sit behind the wheel of the smashed Porsche Spyder that Dean was driving when he died.

~~~

After piano virtuoso Franz Liszt gave a recital, a woman fan stripped the seat cover from the chair he had sat on to keep as a souvenir.

~~~

In the nineteenth century Italian princess Christine Belgiojoso had a lover mummified after he died and kept the mummy in her kitchen cupboard.

UNTRIBUTES

Hey, thanks for all you've done, but please put down that doughnut and accept these bad rewards for good accomplishments:

1. John Garand, the Canadian who invented the semiautomatic rifle named for him, a weapon that was a major reason the Allies won World War II, was never paid royalties for his invention.

2. Walter Botts, famous by visage though not name, was the tall, distinguished model who posed for the drawing that became a national symbol, Uncle Sam.

Although he was the man who literally personified army recruiting (with the Uncle Sam "I want you" posters), Botts's veteran pension was denied.

3. Prudential Life Insurance Company dropped its slogan "Own a Piece of the Rock" after Rock Hudson came out as gay (and later died of complications from AIDS).

Jazz great Louis Armstrong was asked if he was bothered by all the impressions other performers did of his style. He said he didn't mind because "a lot of cats copy the Mona Lisa, but people still line up to see the original."

~~~~

A plastics manufacturer put out a life-size, inflatable plastic doll of the Rolling Stones' Brian Jones as a pool toy. Jones drowned in a swimming pool.

~~~~

Aztec Emperor Montezuma was honored by the poorest of his subjects, who picked the lice from their bodies and sent them to their beloved ruler as a sign of adoration.

~~~~

A nineteenth-century clockmaker, Felix Meier, constructed a two-ton clock to honor the presidents of the United States. On the hour, George Washington rose from his chair and held out the Declaration of Independence while the other presidents paraded before him.

~~~~

A wealthy salesman set up his own town in the northwestern state of Washington and named it to honor his favorite president, calling his town George.

~~~~

Movie star Ava Gardner had an island named after her. To promote the 1957 film *The Little Hut,* a small island in Fiji was renamed Ava Ava and leased to a contest winner.

WHAT DO THESE FAMOUS PEOPLE HAVE IN COMMON?

President Calvin Coolidge; jazz great Louis Armstrong; New York Yankees owner George Steinbrenner; film mogul Louis B. Mayer; playwright Neil Simon; composer Stephen Foster; writers Nathaniel Hawthorne, Ann Landers, and Abigail Van Buren; bandleader Mitch Miller; and gangster Meyer Lansky?

They were all born on the 4th of July.

Four funny people who had nothing to do with rock 'n' roll but were pictured on the cover of the Beatles' *Sgt. Pepper's Lonely Hearts Club Band* album anyway: W. C. Fields, Lenny Bruce, Laurel and Hardy.

Baseball slugger Dave Kingman was as bad in the field as he was good at the plate. In one game, he threw a ball wildly into the Chicago Cubs dugout with such force that the ball bounced through a back door and into the bathroom toilet.

Newspaper columnist Mike Royko suggested that if Kingman was ever sent to the hall of fame for his slugging, "they should put the toilet bowl in there too."

CHAPTER 7

Kiss, kiss, stab, stab

What famous people say about each other

Who was that pitching wedge I saw you with last night? She was a famous star, who found (like so many others) that she wasn't her own worst enemy—other stars were.

STAR SLINGS, GLITZY ARROWS

Susan Sarandon: "Mel Gibson is somewhere to the right of Attila the Hun. He's beautiful, but only on the outside."

~~~~~

Capucine: "Cary Grant had charm, and that was about all. He was cold, paranoid, and cheap."

~~~~~

Composer Frédéric Chopin, about the woman writer with the man's name, George Sand: "What a repellent woman that Sand is. Is she really a woman? I am very much inclined to doubt it."

You probably won't be surprised to learn that Chopin then had an affair with Sand until she broke it off.

Ava Gardner about ex-husband Frank Sinatra after the singer married the svelter actress Mia Farrow: "I always knew he'd end up in bed with a boy."

~~~~~

Frank Sinatra, about Elvis: "His kind of music is deplorable, a rancid-smelling aphrodisiac."

~~~~~

Robert Montgomery: "Costarring with Greta Garbo does not constitute an introduction."

~~~~~

Actor Sterling Hayden: "There is not enough money in Hollywood to lure me into making another picture with Joan Crawford, and I like money."

~~~~~

Actor Kris Kristofferson: "Working with Barbra Streisand is pretty stressful. It's like sitting down to a picnic in the middle of a freeway."

~~~~~

Political pundit Jack Germond about John McLaughlin, host of TV's *The McLaughlin Group*, of which Germond was a long-sitting if grumpy member: "As the program grew more successful, McLaughlin became ever more difficult to abide. His ego, always greater than seemed justified by his charm or achievements, swelled to enormous proportions. He began to behave as if he could do the program with four clothing-store dummies."

Robert Mitchum: "I gave up being serious about making pictures around the time I made a film with Greer Garson and she took 125 takes to say no."

~

Melanie Griffith about working with James Woods: "It is like being pregnant. At first you are happy. Then you think it was a mistake. And in the end you want it to be over."

~

Tennis great Pete Sampras about why he didn't want to date singing star Barbra Streisand. "She's what I call a pitching wedge. She looks good from about 150 yards away."

~

English writer Evelyn Waugh about English politician Randolph Churchill, who'd had a lung removed: "It was announced that the trouble was not malignant. It was a typical triumph of modern science to find the only part of Randolph that was not malignant and remove it."

PRAISE, FAINT AND OTHERWISE

Gene Kelly: "If Fred Astaire is the Cary Grant of dance, I'm the Marlon Brando."

~

Advertising maverick Jerry Della Femina about why he wouldn't go to work on Ronald Reagan's reelection campaign: "I don't sell products that wake up grumpy in the morning and press a button and kill everybody."

Movie producer Brian Grazer about working on a film with star Eddie Murphy: "Eddie is an elusive guy. He is hard to pin down. He's in his trailer and you can't get in. Or he's at home and not taking calls. (In comparison) if you're on Steve Martin's good side, you're in there for life. Arnie, Cruise, Hanks, they're all easy to work with."

~~~

Jazz great Quincy Jones about singer Michael Jackson: "He's a very nice person. He's not the weirdo people think he is."

~~~

NFL lineman Mike Fanning after meeting pop artist Andy Warhol: "I just want to tell you something. Andy Warhol shows up in Tulsa, he gets his ass kicked."

~~~

Burt Reynolds on director Paul Thomas Anderson: "Most film-makers today have no sense of the history of our business, but he knows every shot John Ford made. I remember the first shot in *Boogie Nights,* one of the longest shots in history. And I, being the irascible old type I am sometimes, said, 'Have you timed this? Is this longer than *Citizen Kane*?' And he said, 'Oh yes. It's three seconds longer.'"

~~~

John Huston: "The trouble with Bogart is he thinks he's Bogart."

English wit P. G. Wodehouse describing dinners at Hearst Castle, with patriarch William Randolph sitting in the middle of a long table on one side and Marion Davies on the other: "The longer you are there, the further you get from the middle.

"I sat on Marion's right the first night, then found myself being edged further and further away till I got to the extreme end, when I thought it time to leave. Another day and I should have been feeding on the floor."

~~~

Jean Cocteau about a fellow French writer: "Victor Hugo was a madman who thought he was Victor Hugo."

CHAPTER 8

Only a wife can keep you away from Howard Stern

Family tales of the famous

What can you say if you're the president of the United States and someone sneaks a pony up to the second floor of the White House on the elevator?

If you're President Teddy Roosevelt, all you can say is: They're family.

~~~

Chubby Checker spawned a huge dance craze with his pop song "The Twist." But the song came first, before there was a dance to go with it. How did Chubby come up with the dance?

He asked his seven-year-old brother, Spencer, what he thought the Twist would look like as a dance. What Spencer showed him became the moves that moved a nation.

~~~

When actress Nicole Kidman was a little girl, her feminist mother refused to buy her a Barbie doll. So Nicole did what any self-respecting daughter would do: She went out and stole one.

Before scientist Charles Darwin became famous for his theory of evolution, he spent eight years studying barnacles, keeping ten thousand of the briny creatures in his family home.

Darwin's children grew so used to a barnacle-infused home life that when one of his sons visited a friend he inquired, "Where does your father do his barnacles?"

~~~

When Theodore Roosevelt was president, his five kids had the run of the White House. When they weren't sneaking ponies up the elevator, one of their favorite games was to take trays from the pantry and ride them down the stairs.

~~~

Sir Thomas More, sixteenth-century English chancellor, had progressive views on marriage. He maintained that prospective couples should see each other naked before agreeing to wed.

When a friend requested permission to marry one of More's daughters, he led him up to her bedroom and swept aside the sheets so the prospective groom could see what he was getting.

~~~

Before humorist Will Rogers was born in Oologah, Oklahoma, his family lived in a house that was part frame, part logs.

To deliver baby Will, his mother moved into the log portion of the house so that her son could be born in a log cabin like her hero, Abe Lincoln.

Movie director Garry Marshall talking about his working relationship with his sister, movie director Penny Marshall: "Penny sat through a four-hour version of *Beaches,* and I sat through her 4½-hour first cut of *Awakenings*. Only your family will watch first cuts like that."

Garry had a small role in Penny's baseball film, *A League of Their Own*.

"Penny gave me the part because I work cheap," Garry explained.

When Jules Leotard was a baby, his parents hung him upside down from a trapeze bar to stop his crying.

He went on to become the most famous aerialist of nineteenth-century Europe and inventor of the costume that lives on after him.

WHAT DO THESE ACTORS HAVE IN COMMON?

Paul Newman, John Houseman, Carrie Fisher, Kathie Lee Gifford, Jamie Lee Curtis, Joan Collins, Michael Landon, and Kevin Kline.

They all have Jewish fathers and Catholic or Protestant mothers.

When President Warren Harding died in office, vice president Calvin Coolidge was vacationing at his Plymouth Notch home. Coolidge's father, who was a notary public, became the only father to administer the oath of office to his son.

~~~

As a movie star, Sophia Loren was the epitome of the voluptuous woman. But no one saw that coming. As a child, Sophia's family nicknamed her Toothpick.

~~~

Science-fiction writer H. G. Wells blamed his mother for making him short (five-foot-five), claiming she retarded his growth by confining him to a small bed.

~~~

As a boy, religious leader Martin Luther and his entire family slept together naked.

~~~

Ex-drummer Lenny Hart managed the Grateful Dead in the band's early days. He got the job because his son Mickey was the Dead's drummer. Then Lenny stole thousands of dollars from his son's band.

"He was an absolute rotten human being," Mickey said after Lenny's death. "I'm ashamed that he was my father. But he was a superb drummer."

~~~

Movie star Katharine Hepburn used her brother's birth date as her own for years.

Singer Shawn Colvin's album *Whole New You* was a response to a whole new writing challenge: the birth of a daughter.

Very few songs are written about having a baby.

"It's not very well-plowed territory," Colvin said. "You don't have the experience of going to your favorite artist and listening to their 'just had a kid' record. Fell in love or just got dumped? You get a lot of those. We all know how to do those records."

~~~

When Jimmy Stewart starred in the controversial movie *Anatomy of a Murder*, the star's own father took out a newspaper ad urging people not to see his son's "dirty picture."

~~~

When Ferenc Molnár became a successful playwright, he lived in a hotel in Vienna. One day a group of relatives visited him, hoping he'd share his good fortune with them. Molnár threw a dinner and arranged for a photographer to take a group portrait.

The next day he showed the portrait to the hotel doorman with instructions that none of the people in the photo ever be let back in.

~~~

New Yorker writer and critic Alexander Woollcott had no children, but did serve as godfather to the children of his celebrated friends—nineteen times.

When he became godfather of the child of actress Helen Hayes and playwright Charles MacArthur, Woollcott sighed, "Always a godfather, never a god."

FAMILY REUNIONS

Famous people who were connected to other famous people somehow:

1. Elvis Presley was a direct descendant of Abraham Lincoln's great-great grandfather, Isaiah Harrison.

2. Tom Hanks is a direct descendant of Nancy Hanks, Abraham Lincoln's mother.

3. Ginger Rogers's grandmother on her mother's side was a descendent of George Washington. The actress was also a sort-of cousin of Rita Hayworth. Ginger's aunt married Rita's uncle.

4. Actress Holly Hunter's cousin is baseball player Tim Salmon.

5. Actor William Hurt's ex-wife Heidi is the daughter of TV band leader Skitch Henderson.

6. Actress Anjelica Huston was the half-sister-in-law of actress Virginia Madsen.

7. Actor Matt Dillon's grand-uncles were both famous artists: Uncle Alex Raymond created the cartoon strips "Flash Gordon" and "Jungle Jim," while uncle Jim Raymond drew "Blondie" for Chic Young for forty years.

Comic actress and director Penny Marshall developed her comic sensibility growing up in an argumentative Bronx family.

"If someone said, 'Let's all get into the car and go down to the malt shop,' everyone would be saying, 'Ooooh,' and I'd be saying, 'How far is the car?' That's where I'm coming from."

～～～

Playwright Eugene O'Neill requested that his epic play "Long Day's Journey Into Night" not be produced until twenty-five years after his death. Why? The play reveals too many of the O'Neill family secrets.

～～～

Singer Toni Braxton's parents did not allow her to listen to pop music or wear anything but simple dresses until her mid-teens.

"We couldn't go to the movies. It was a sin. It was thought that it promoted witchcraft. We couldn't go roller skating. We had to wear long dresses, hats, no open-toed shoes. Show no nakedness."

But the singer claimed that the racy outfits she wore onstage were not a reaction against her strict upbringing but an effort to compensate for being short (five-foot-two).

"As a little girl I always wanted to be like the black Marilyn Monroe," Braxton said. "She was so sexy. I think when you're short and you show skin, it makes you look taller, and it gives you the illusion that you're like Cindy Crawford, that you're sexy and grand like that."

The daughter could write and the father ran one of the biggest publishing firms, but they were in two different fields.

Father Richard Simon ran the book publisher, Simon and Schuster, while daughter Carly Simon wrote a lot of songs. Remember Carly's "You're So Vain," which half the famous people in the world thought she wrote about them?

When Alan Alda's TV show *M*A*S*H* became a hit, he got his dad, Robert Alda, three guest spots and his brother Anthony one.

Rocker Eddie Money's record company wanted him to appear on TV's scandal show *Behind the Music*, but he refused for family reasons:

"I don't think my kids wanted to know that their father had a drug overdose or was married to somebody else," he said. "So I passed.

"Then they wanted to me to do *Howard Stern*. And my wife says, 'You're not going on with Howard Stern. I can't stand him.'"

CHAPTER 9

Unstandard operating procedures

Unusual ways celebrities have gotten the job done

Novelist Graham Greene had an original approach to his books: He wrote two hundred words a day, every day, but only two hundred.

If he was in the middle of a sentence when he reached word two hundred, he would stop right . . .

Let's take a look at other unusual work habits of famous people.

At his summer house, inventor Thomas Edison amused himself by installing a variety of clever devices. One of them was a turnstile that blocked the path up to the house. Anyone walking to the house had to rotate the turnstile to get through.

Each time they turned the stile, they pumped eight gallons of water into the tank on Edison's roof.

The principles of manipulative advertising were understood long before Madison Avenue turned lies into an art form.

In the tenth century, Norwegian explorer Eric the Red discovered a barren island of glacial rock, which he named Greenland to lure people to his colony.

~~~

Comic writer Robert Benchley was struggling over one of his stories for the *New Yorker* in the early, madcap days of that magazine. After an hour of musing, he typed the single word "The" on a clean piece of paper.

He stared at the word, fretted, reconsidered, then got up and went drinking.

Several hours later, he returned to his office and finished the sentence: "... hell with it."

~~~

Composer Johannes Brahms stood during musical performances because it helped him concentrate better.

Also up-standing for art: Victor Hugo, who wrote *Les Miserables* and *The Hunchback of Notre Dame* standing up.

Hugo was able to produce such mammoth novels because he slept fewer than four hours a night.

~~~

Kirk Douglas earned $50,000 for saying the only English word at the end of a Japanese TV commercial: "Coffee."

That's a word you or I probably could have been talked into saying for ten, maybe twelve thou.

WHAT THEY WOULD HAVE DONE IF THEY HADN'T DONE WHAT THEY DID

1. President Harry Truman would have been "a piano player in a bawdy house."

2. Movie star Paul Newman: a sporting goods salesman.

3. Movie star Robert Redford: a painter.

4. Singer Pat Boone: a high school teacher.

5. Songwriter Burt Bacharach: a football player.

6. Actor Spencer Tracy: a priest.

7. Another would-be priest: Russian dictator Joseph Stalin, who was booted out of a seminary for reading the subversive writings of Karl Marx and Charles Dickens.

In the movie *The Goodbye Girl,* Marsha Mason delivers a long speech as she walks down the hall from her room to Richard Dreyfuss's room.

The movie's set designer timed her speech, then built the hallway precisely one Marsha-walk long, so Mason could deliver the entire speech without having to stop walking.

In a memorable scene from the western *Shane*, villain Jack Palance doesn't ride into town on his horse (like every other western bad guy) but menacingly walks his horse down the main street.

Where did this unusual idea for a gunslinger scene come from?

Palance was a bad rider. He looked so bad riding the horse into town, that director George Stevens gave up and told him to walk the horse instead.

Of such inadequacies are great moments sometimes born.

~~~

To dramatize the violence in the thriller *Bullitt*, director Peter Yates made sure only one thing in the movie would be colored red: blood.

Even the Coke signs and stop signs were changed from red to brown.

"You recognize them as red because you've seen them as red all your life," the movie's production designer explained. "You don't think about it. But they weren't red."

~~~

Richard Burton: "When I played drunks I had to remain sober because I didn't know how to play them when I was drunk."

~~~

President William Howard Taft lost badly in his bid for reelection. But he took the loss philosophically, commenting, "No candidate was ever elected ex-president by such a large majority."

Comic actor John Belushi did most of his own stunts in movies. But that last gag in *Animal House,* where Belushi rides a banner from a rooftop down to the street, that was a pretty dangerous stunt. How did Belushi manage it?

Got himself wired on cocaine first. Considering what killed Belushi, kind of cuts off the laughs, doesn't it?

～～～

When Richard Benjamin directed the comedy *Made in America,* he was about to film a scene with star Ted Danson and a real bear. Benjamin made the mistake of asking the animal trainer if the bear was safe.

"Well, he is a bear," the trainer explained. "If he wanted to go through this whole crew, you couldn't stop him."

"Should we tell Ted this?" Benjamin wondered aloud.

The director did, but not until *after* they'd shot the scene.

～～～

From dancing star Eleanor Powell, about how hard she worked on her pictures: "The blood came right through our pink ballet slippers. And when we took our slippers off that night, they had big buckets of ice. I lost four toenails on the right foot."

～～～

Alfred Hitchcock, who made some of the greatest suspense movies of all time, was challenged by a French customs officer who didn't recognize the filmmaker. When Hitchcock listed his profession as "producer," the officer questioned, "What do you produce?"

Hitchcock's response: "Gooseflesh."

Alexandre Dumas, author of *The Three Musketeers*, wrote numerous plays and books, assisted by a staff of ghostwriters.

Once he asked his son, "Have you read my new book yet?"

"No," his son replied. "Have you?"

Dumas also developed an unusual system of sorting out his work: He wrote all his poems on yellow paper, his novels on blue paper, and his nonfiction on rose-colored paper.

Also color-coordinated: Jullien, a celebrated English conductor of the nineteenth century, employed an unusual color-coding system to lead the symphony—gold batons for Mozart, silver for Mendelssohn, and a bejeweled baton to perform Beethoven.

Hungarian writer Ferenc Molnár developed the routine of working all night and sleeping till afternoon. He was forced out of this routine early one morning when ordered by a judge to appear as a witness in a lawsuit.

As Molnár stepped out into the early-morning crowds of Budapest, he was amazed to see the streets filled with people hurrying to work.

"Good heavens," he exclaimed, "are all these people witnesses in this fool case?"

Famous fashion designer Rudi Gernreich realized that his profession offered a unique kind of job protection: "A homosexual man is not thrown out of his profession because he's a hairdresser or a stage designer. People sort of feel more secure that he is. But if a riveter in a defense plant is a homosexual, he'll keep that very quiet because if he's discovered he may lose his job."

When writer and bon vivant Wilson Mizner worked as manager of a seedy Manhattan hotel in 1907, he posted two house rules in the lobby: 1. No opium smoking in the elevator. 2. Carry out your own dead.

When the McGuire Sisters broke into the music business, they were so naive that for six months they carried their first record contract with them wherever they went.

When singer Janis Joplin signed her first big recording contract with a major label, she didn't think a signature was enough, so she offered to sleep with the corporate executive to close the deal.

How great are the labors of art? Depends upon the opportunity, as actor Peter Ustinov observed: "If Botticelli were alive today, he'd be working for *Vogue*."

HARD WORKERS

1. Composer Robert Schumann wrote 125 songs in one year, half of his total production.

2. The novel *Gone With the Wind* was such a hit that author Margaret Mitchell had to hire two secretaries just to answer fan mail.

3. Songwriter Cole Porter had three musicals open on Broadway in five weeks.

4. George Rogers Clark, who founded Louisville, was the most efficient Revolutionary War general. He was the only one to win every battle he fought.

5. When the great Nolan Ryan pitched for the Rangers, he spent the '91 off-season autographing 90,000 baseballs, photos, and posters. Made almost $2 million doing it.

6. Artist Pablo Picasso ensured not only his own fortune but also that of numerous gallery owners, auctioneers, and collectors by producing during his life 14,000 paintings, 34,000 illustrations, and 100,000 prints.

7. While in a Chicago jail, gangster Al Capone ran his criminal empire by phone, using the warden's office.

8. When Cesar Ritz opened his great hotel in Paris in 1898, he displayed his obsession with detail by sleeping a night in each room to test each mattress for comfort and quality.

Mark Twain wrote most of his books in bed, propped up on pillows. He even conducted interviews with newspaper reporters while in bed.

When his wife suggested this might be an embarrassment, Twain offered to have the other bed made up for the reporter.

~~~

When he was starting out as a mystery writer, Erle Stanley Gardner was paid for his stories by the word, so he padded them whenever he could.

"At three cents a word, every time I say 'bang' in a story I get three cents," he explained. "If you think I'm going to finish a gun battle while my hero's got 15 cents worth of unexploded ammunition in his gun, you're nuts."

~~~

Architect Frank Lloyd Wright had this good advice for people starting out in business: "The physician can bury his mistakes, but the architect can only advise his client to plant vines. So they should go as far as possible from home to build their first buildings."

~~~

Rock 'n' roll's Frank Zappa defined the qualifications for rock journalism as "people who can't write interviewing people who can't talk for people who can't read."

CHAPTER 10

Now that you're eighty years old, here's your sixteen cents

Fame and money

The comedy team Abbott and Costello bought a $100,000 insurance policy (with Lloyds of London, who else?) to protect them in case anyone in the audience died laughing.

Is it possible to die laughing? Please, don't make me laugh.

Stars have the same relationship to money as the rest of us—they just have that relationship to *more* money.

~~~

When a movie producer asked Igor Stravinsky to write the score for his film, the composer demanded significantly more money than another composer had earned in a similar project.

"He had talent," Stravinsky explained. "I have not, so for me the work is more difficult."

While suing his accountants for mismanagement of funds, pop singer Elton John bragged that living expenses cost him $2.15 million a month, although he could not explain to the court what one person could spend so much money on.

~~~~

When Jackie Gleason was a struggling young comedian, he played a nightclub at an ocean resort. Not having enough money to pay the rent at the boardinghouse, Gleason tossed his suitcase out the window, then strolled out through the lobby wearing his swimsuit and carrying a towel so as not to arouse the landlady's suspicions.

Several years later and much more successful, Gleason was passing through that coastal town and decided to pay off his debt. When he walked into the boarding house, the landlady shrieked in recognition. "My lord," she cried, "I thought you had drowned."

~~~~

When the wealthy magnate Andrew Carnegie was criticized by a socialist for the unequal distribution of wealth, Carnegie figured out his total value, then divided it by the world population and told an assistant to give the socialist 16 cents.

"That's his share of my wealth," Carnegie asserted.

~~~~

Football star Brett Favre: "My dad, in thirty years of coaching and teaching, never made, altogether, what I make in two weeks. That's scary."

When Arthur Conan Doyle was a successful writer, he was rehearsing a production of one of his plays. A young, unknown actor suggested that the two of them pool their incomes, then each take half for the rest of his life.

The writer laughed off the idea. The actor went on to become the incredibly successful and even wealthier Charlie Chaplin.

Movie star Gary Cooper found he could save plenty of money by paying for everything he bought with checks. Many of the people he paid wouldn't cash the check because they wanted to keep it as an autographed souvenir.

Singer Bing Crosby left a clause in his will stating that his sons could not collect their share of his fortune until they were in their 80s.

When composer Claude Debussy got married, he was flat broke. On his wedding day, he gave a piano lesson to pay for his bride's breakfast.

Movie mogul Sam Goldwyn produced *The Best Years of Our Lives,* a serious film with dim box office prospects. But as he explained, "I don't care if it doesn't make a nickel. I just want every man, woman, and child in America to see it."

An infamous oil speculator back in the late 1800s had a great nickname: John "Bet-You-a-Million" Gates. He once bet another wealthy man, John Drake of the Drake University family, $11,000 over whose bread, dunked in coffee, would draw more flies.

Gates won the bet. No surprise to "Bet-a-Million" and not much of a gamble really, because before he made the wager he had mixed six spoons of sugar into his coffee.

Banker J. P. Morgan once sent back a sealed box to a jeweler with a check for $4,000, which was $1,000 less than the jeweler had asked for the price of a pearl.

Along with the return box came a note from Morgan that if the jeweler would accept the lower price, he should return the box with the seal intact. If not, return the check and keep the box.

The jeweler refused the $4,000 and opened the box, expecting to get his pearl back. Instead, he found inside a check for $5,000.

A White House visitor asked President Calvin Coolidge for a cigar so he could give it to a friend who collected cigar bands from famous people.

Coolidge took a cigar from his desktop box, removed the band, gave the visitor the band and kept the cigar.

When communist theorist Karl Marx and his bride, Jenny, went on their honeymoon, they left their money in an open strongbox in their hotel room so anyone who needed money could take it.

~~~

Star Cary Grant didn't like a picture he was filming, *The Awful Truth*, so he offered the studio chief $5,000 to take him out of the movie.

When director Leo McCarey heard about Grant's reverse bribe, he offered to chip in another $10,000 to get rid of Grant.

The movie became one of Grant's biggest hits.

~~~

One hundred years ago, the bishop of Chicago denounced actress Sarah Bernhardt as the "whore of Babylon." Her response? She sent the bishop a check for $200 and a note of thanks.

"I am accustomed when I bring an attraction to your town to spend $400 on advertising," the actress explained. "As you have done half the advertising for me, I herewith enclose $200 for your parish."

~~~

Writer and cartoonist James Thurber kept no records of how much money he had in his bank account. Not surprisingly, he overdrew his account.

When his banker explained to Thurber that he had to keep track of his money, the *New Yorker* cartoonist, sounding surprised, said, "I thought that was your business."

When Ted Williams played for the Boston Red Sox, he gave all of his 1946 World Series check as a tip to the clubhouse boy.

~~~

While they were at a society party in Manhattan, poet e. e. cummings realized he was flat broke and needed to raise enough money so he and his wife could take the subway home.

An original thinker, cummings sold the privilege of stamping on his hat to a wealthy man for $5 and took a taxi home.

~~~

Studio boss Adolph Zukor once slighted playwright George S. Kaufman by offering him only $30,000 for movie rights to one of his plays. Kaufman sent a wire back offering Zukor $40,000 for Paramount Studios.

~~~

Scientists Marie and Pierre Curie, who discovered radio-activity, refused to patent their findings or make any money from it at all.

~~~

In 1965, Soupy Sales's TV show played to kids but was also popular with sarcastic teenagers. On one show, the comic told his younger viewers to send him "those little green pieces of paper" they would find in their fathers' wallets.

They did, and the network suspended Soupy's show.

While on the run from the law after robbing a bank, Jesse James and his gang spent a night at a rundown farmhouse. The widow who lived there shared what little food she had, then told Jesse she was going to lose the farm because a banker was coming out to collect $1,400 she didn't have.

Jesse gave the woman the money. The next day, James and his men waited until the banker made the collection, then they robbed the banker and rode off into legend. The woman kept her farm.

Soul singer Joe Cocker made a lot of money in his career, which is important because he also gave a lot away, often giving friends who wanted to buy a house tens of thousands of dollars for the down payment. This hurt him when he got into trouble with the government and didn't have the money to pay back taxes.

Elvis's manager, Colonel Tom Parker, once offered to sell anecdotes about the King to a writer at $2,500 per tale.

Although his father was a millionaire, John Paul Getty made his first personal million at the age of twenty-four, after two years in the oil prospecting business. Then he retired.

The young Getty came back a few years later when he realized there were still many millions to be made and he had nothing else to do.

CHAPTER 11

Tom Cruise almost became a what?

Infamous surprises

It's not that famous people do surprising things. More that people who do surprising things often become famous.

Perhaps they heeded this advice from poet Alice Walker: "Expect nothing. Live frugally on surprise."

You probably thought that when the great *Saturday Night Live* comic John Belushi was in high school, he was class clown or voted Most Likely to Goof Off.

No so. Belushi was cocaptain of his high school football team and elected homecoming king.

Actor George Clooney is known as a practical joker among his Hollywood crowd. At parties, he would borrow someone's camera, then run to the bathroom and take a photo of his butt, knowing that when the unsuspecting camera owner had the film developed he was in for a rear surprise.

When Jack Norworth was honored with a special day at Ebbets Field, home of the Brooklyn Dodgers, it was the first time he'd ever been inside a baseball park.

What's odd about that? Norworth wrote the lyrics to the second-most-often played song in ball parks: "Take Me Out to the Ballgame."

〜〜

At age fourteen, Tom Cruise enrolled in a seminary to become a priest. He dropped out after one year.

〜〜

All actors dread that moment: A play ends and no one applauds.

It happened to stage actress Helen Hayes, when she turned in what she thought was her best performance as Mary Stuart, Queen of Scots. At the end of the play, Mary was left alone onstage, in the cell waiting for her beheading.

The curtain fell. Not a sound from the audience. No applause, none.

"I changed into my street clothes and went out the back door of the theater," Hayes recalled. "That long alley on a drizzly night was filled with people. The audience had moved back there.

"And as I went out and down the little steps from the door to the ground and walked through the crowd, that's when they applauded."

Has any actor ever received a more wonderful tribute?

Maureen O'Sullivan, who played Jane in the Tarzan movies, claimed that Cheetah and the apes were all homosexuals, "eager to wrap their paws around Johnny Weissmuller's thighs. They were jealous of me, and I loathed them."

~~~~

The Grateful Dead once proposed recording thirty minutes of air as background upon which they would then record their music.

They dropped the project when a producer convinced them that it was against the rules of the musicians' union to record air.

~~~~

Golfer Lee Trevino was a trick-shot artist who invented handicaps to win bets. Among his many amazing golf feats: winning a round without a golf club, using only a soda bottle to hit the ball.

~~~~

No one at the Walt Disney animation shop thought one of their early cartoons, *The Three Little Pigs,* was going to be anything special. But it became a surprise hit.

Disney was so unprepared for the sudden popularity of the film's song, "Who's Afraid of the Big Bad Wolf?" that he didn't even have sheet music written.

When music stores around the nation were besieged for the sheet music, Disney had to send musicians into a movie theater to copy the words and music from the screen.

WHAT DO THESE FAMOUS PEOPLE HAVE IN COMMON?

Singers Neil Diamond, Lena Horne, and Barbra Streisand; actors Richard Dreyfuss, Louis Gossett Jr., Steve Buscemi, Mary Tyler Moore, and Adam Sandler; filmmakers Woody Allen and James L. Brooks; Carole King; Larry King; Alan King; and the author of this book (who is an example, in the extreme, of localized fame).

They were all born in Brooklyn.

Actress Angela Lansbury played Laurence Harvey's manipulative mother in the 1962 thriller *The Manchurian Candidate*. In real life she was only three years older than Harvey.

What comedian Dick Gregory promised to do if elected president in 1968: "Paint the White House black."

Makes you stop and wonder: Why is the White House white?

Shouldn't it be red, white, and blue for the flag? Or green for the forests we have left? Or even purple for the mountains' majesty?

Why do I suspect that the White House is white because the contractor had some extra white paint he had to unload?

When James Naismith invented basketball in 1891, how many players were allowed on a team?

Up to fifty players on each side, all on the court at the same time. It wasn't until six years later that the teams were cut down to five.

~~~

When poet Robert Frost taught a writing class in 1926, he gave his students one unusual assignment for their final: "Do anything that you think would please me."

One student signed his name to a blank piece of paper and turned it in as his finished test. He got the only A in the class.

Reminds me of that philosophy professor who placed a rock on his desk and challenged his students to write a meta-physical essay proving that the rock did *not* exist.

The student who aced the assignment wrote a single sentence: "What rock?"

~~~

In the 1932 national track and field championships, Babe Didrikson entered the meet as a one-woman track team. She won five events and tied for a sixth, scoring more team points than all of the athletes in the second-place team put together.

~~~

Transcendentalist philosopher Ralph Waldo Emerson was confronted by a religious cultist, who predicted that the world was coming to an end.

Emerson was unperturbed, declaring, "No doubt we will get on very well without it."

When George Harrison was stabbed in his house by a crazed attacker, the ex-Beatle had an unusual defense: He shouted, "Hare Krishna! Hare Krishna!" at the knife-wielding madman.

Although the meditative chant is more typically used to achieve inner bliss, Harrison thought it would disorient the attacker.

~~~

When hockey great Phil Esposito was a young member of the Canadian team sent to play the Russians in Moscow, he and his roommate searched their hotel room for hidden microphones.

Finding a small, round piece of metal imbedded in the floor under a rug, they assumed that was the bug. They pried out the piece of metal, only to hear a tremendous crash from the room below. They had removed the anchor that held the chandelier to the ceiling beneath them.

~~~

When Birdie Tebbetts was fired as manager of the Milwaukee Braves in 1963, he left behind two sealed envelopes in the manager's desk. Both envelopes carried this warning: "Open in emergency only."

Tebbetts's successor, Bobby Bragan, found the letters and opened the first one in his second year, when he was struggling with a bad team. Inside were these words from Tebbetts: "Blame it on me."

A year later, Bragan still hadn't turned the team around, and he opened the second emergency envelope. Inside was a simple message from Tebbetts: "Prepare two letters."

When James Joyce was writing *Finnegan's Wake,* he dictated some of the book to playwright Samuel Beckett. When someone knocked on the door, Joyce called, "Come in," and Beckett wrote those words into the manuscript.

Reading the draft back later, James wondered what that "Come in" was for, since it didn't fit what was happening in the story at the time—at least as far as anyone could tell, which wasn't far, and if you've tried to read *Finnegan's Wake,* you know what I mean.

"You said that," Beckett explained.

Joyce considered the error, then said, "Let it stand."

~~~

When Pat Boone recorded a cover of Little Richard's rock 'n' roll classic "Tutti Frutti," he was embarrassed by the lyric "Boy, you don't know what she's doing to me." So he changed the line and sang, "Pretty little Suzie is the girl for me."

~~~

Steve McQueen loved riding motorcycles so much that in one scene of the World War II prison film *The Great Escape,* he put on a German uniform and portrayed one of the soldiers chasing a prisoner who had escaped on a stolen motorcycle.

What was strange about this? McQueen was also playing the escaped prisoner he was chasing.

~~~

When politician Adlai Stevenson was twelve years old, he accidentally shot his cousin to death.

Soul singer Bill Medley had that deep, romantic voice that made the Righteous Brothers' "You've Lost That Loving Feeling" the most romantic song of a decade.

But when Medley was in his high school choir, he sang tenor. Then his voice changed.

~~~

In the 1924 Olympics, the great distance runner Paavo Nurmi won gold in both the 1,500 meter and the 5,000. After the day's triumphs, Nurmi refused to take the athletes' bus back to Paris. Instead, he walked back from the stadium, six miles to his hotel.

~~~

For a Father's Day gift when he was fifty-six, President Richard Nixon received a custom-made blue surfboard from his daughters.

Historians have found no record that Richard Nixon ever surfed—unless those missing seventeen minutes on the White House tapes were from the president's Beach Boys LP.

~~~

In 1876, a large force of cavalry, mountaineers, adventurers, and fighters gathered at Fort Laramie to battle the Sioux. There were 1,500 men and one woman: Calamity Jane.

~~~

In 1970, when Henry Kissinger was awarded the Nobel Peace Prize, two members of the Nobel committee resigned in protest. That's two out of five.

The producers of the movie *Woodstock* got into a huge dispute with Warner Bros. movie studio about how long the final cut of the film would be. The studio wanted a shorter film so it could play more times a day in theaters and make more money. The filmmakers wanted a longer film that would be truer to the Woodstock concert.

Alvin Lee, lead singer of the band Ten Years After, heard that other Woodstock performers had started a telegram campaign demanding that Warner Bros. leave the film alone. Lee sent off a telegram to join the protest.

Only problem for Lee and the band: There was no protest. His was the only telegram.

The studio reacted by cutting out Ten Years After from the film. But their performance was saved by their manager (who also managed Joe Cocker), who told the studio that if Ten Years After was out, so was his big star.

The studio backed down because it didn't want to lose Joe Cocker's performance, one of the wildest at the festival and in the film.

Peter the Great of Russia was loved by his soldiers, and he returned the feelings with devotion to those who served him. At the age of fifty-three, the czar jumped from his horse and dove into an icy river to rescue drowning soldiers. He got hypothermia as a result and died from it.

Dr. Seuss, the greatest children's book writer of all time, didn't like having children around the house. "You raise them," he used to say, "I'll entertain them."

When he married a divorced woman who had two young girls, the writer convinced her to send them off to boarding school so he wouldn't have young kids running around the house while he was trying to write books for young kids.

～～～

Were the 1901–05 Michigan Wolverines the greatest dynasty in college football? With a 55-1-1 record, they outscored opponents 2821 to 42.

The Wolverines got the job done because they had a competitive advantage: Their star running back had already played for and graduated from another college.

Didn't that violate the rules of college football? "Weren't any rules back then," legendary Wolverine coach Fielding Yost explained.

～～～

Philosopher Bertrand Russell made an odd discovery: "Whenever I talk with a savant, I feel quite sure that happiness is no longer a possibility. Yet when I talk with my gardener, I'm convinced of the opposite."

CHAPTER 12

Naked Ping-Pong
and the anchovy defense

Odd celebrity quirks

Eighteenth-century English poet William Blake and his wife, Catherine, enjoyed reciting poetry to each other while sitting naked in their garden.

How charming, and if the Blakes had been ordinary naked poetry readers, no one (but a surprised visitor or two) would have known about their unusual habit. But they were famous, so now we all know.

Revealing the peculiarities of the notorious helps put our own eccentricities in perspective.

~

Millionaire Cornelius Vanderbilt always slept with the legs of his bed stuck in dishes of salt to keep evil spirits from attacking him in his sleep.

~

Evangelist Mary Baker Eddy slept in a giant cradle, rocked to sleep by hired boys.

Sigmund Freud's wife, Martha, put the toothpaste on the toothbrush for her husband.

~~~

Comic actor John Belushi would borrow a twenty-dollar bill from new acquaintances so he could judge what they'd be like as friends by how they reacted to his request.

~~~

King Farouk of Egypt had one hundred of his cars painted red, then declared it illegal for anyone else in Egypt to own a red car.

The king also owned huge collections of clocks, bottle caps, and toothpaste tubes.

~~~

Writer Henry Miller liked to play Ping-Pong with naked women. If you have read one of Miller's autobiographical books, such as *Tropic of Cancer,* naked Ping-Pong seems quaint compared with the other games he played.

~~~

Sophia Loren liked to roll her bare feet over a wooden rolling pin while watching TV. That's a comforting image, isn't it?

~~~

The twelfth-century Japanese emperor Sutoku took three years to copy a vast Buddhist text using, instead of ink, his own blood.

Writer Marcel Proust lined his bedroom walls with cork so he could write undisturbed by noise from outside his private world.

~~~

Movie star Clark Gable was a bit touchy about germs, so he showered numerous times each day and shaved his chest and armpits so germs couldn't nest.

~~~

Writer Ernest Hemingway was allergic to strawberries but believed he could overcome the allergy by having sex before he ate them.

Can you imagine the choice a polite hostess faced if she invited Hemingway for dinner and served strawberries for dessert? Did Emily Post have anything to say about how to handle that situation?

~~~

English writer Ian Fleming, creator of James Bond, required guests at his estate to stay off the lawns in the early morning so as not to disturb the dew on the spider webs. It was Fleming's custom to walk about and observe the dewy webs upon rising.

~~~

John Quincy Adams, sixth president of the United States, started each day by bathing au naturel in the Potomac River.

~~~

Chinese artist Huang Erhnan specialized in silk paintings in the 1920s. To create the paintings, he used a unique brush: his tongue.

England's prime minister Winston Churchill found the sound of staplers irksome, so he had his staff fasten all his papers by punching holes in the pages and lashing them together with tape.

When movie star Richard Burton complained that celebrity-buzzing photographers followed him into the bathrooms of Rome, writer Quentin Crisp came up with a unique suggestion: "The solution was not to retreat from view but to learn to urinate with style."

Opera singer Enrico Caruso wore anchovies around his neck to protect his singing voice from the two packs of cigarettes he smoked every day.

Victor Borge, the concert pianist who was also a comedian (or the comedian who was also a concert pianist), kept two concert grands back to back in his Connecticut mansion.

Why did he need two grand pianos, other than the fact that he was rich and could afford them?

"When I do four hands, I run around," he explained. "Or with two hands, I play it twice."

Among the English elite in the early eighteenth century, gentlemen shaved off their own hair, then donned elaborate wigs.

The famous diarist Samuel Pepys came up with an interesting twist on this style: He cut off all his own hair, had it made into a wig, then wore that.

The day after Christmas, movie stars Cary Grant and Clark Gable would swap monogrammed gifts they didn't want.

~~~

When George Washington was president, he ordered that the six white horses in his stables have their teeth brushed every morning. Perhaps he didn't want them to end up with wooden teeth, as he did.

~~~

When millionaire Howard Hughes married movie star Jean Peters, he wouldn't let her shave her legs, so all her publicity photos had to be retouched.

~~~

Movie director Alfred Hitchcock had a habit of falling asleep at Hollywood parties.

At one party, he slept for several hours, then his wife woke him and said it was time to go home.

Noting that it was only one in the morning, Hitchcock argued that they shouldn't leave because their hosts would "think we aren't enjoying ourselves."

CHAPTER 13

We could all be walking around in Jerry Lewis's suits

*Opening up celebrity closets
and trying on their clothes*

From Dennis Rodman taking the offense with T-shirts to Clark Gable's un-shirt, celebrities don't just wear clothes, they wear bees and their neckties go visiting.

～～～

For the final twenty years of her life, poet Emily Dickinson dressed only in white.

～～～

In the movie *It Happened One Night,* Clark Gable takes off his shirt, revealing that he isn't wearing an undershirt. (At the time men in America were undershirt men.)

The movie, and Gable, were such a hit that sales of undershirts dropped 75 percent.

～～～

Even when they were multimillionaires, Henry Ford's wife, Clara, darned the holes in his socks. If they ever got down to his final million, she was prepared to make ends meet.

When Betty Grable and Douglas Fairbanks Jr. starred in the movie *That Lady in Ermine,* she gave him an ermine jockstrap and he gave her an ermine chastity belt.

~~~

Basketball great Dennis Rodman bought T-shirts with these slogans: "I don't mind straight people as long as they act gay in public" and "I'm not gay, but my boyfriend is."

~~~

Exhibiting a fashion sense rare in Hollywood—where the words *fashion* and *sense* are never seen together in public—Katharine Hepburn explained her personal style: "I wear my sort of clothes to save me the trouble of deciding which clothes to wear."

~~~

Frederick the Great of Prussia ordered his soldiers to sew buttons on the sleeves of their coats. Why? To stop them from wiping their noses on their sleeves—and that's how men's jackets got sleeve buttons that don't button.

The next time you see a man wearing a thousand-dollar suit with buttons on the sleeves, you might ask him if he has stopped wiping his nose on his arm yet.

~~~

When Mark Twain returned from a visit to the writer Harriet Beecher Stowe, his wife was angry with him when she saw that he had neglected to wear a necktie.

Twain promptly put a necktie in a box and sent it around to Harriet's house, instructing her to keep it for half an hour (the length of his visit), then return it to him.

Comic actor Jerry Lewis gave away suits rather than have them cleaned. He refused to wear a pair of socks more than once.

~~~

Paul Newman burned his tuxedo on his seventy-fifth birthday, deciding he was through with formality.

~~~

When Virginia Madsen starred in the horror movie *Candyman,* she was covered in bees for a crucial scene.

Production assistants glued Virginia's clothes to her body so the bees couldn't get inside. But some of the glue loosened, and the bees crawled down her dress.

"I had to disrobe so they could vacuum the bees off my body," Madsen said. "The bees are furry, so when they crawl over your skin, it feels like you're getting a facial."

~~~

Beau Brummell, who ruled the conventions of English society in the 1800s, would spend an entire day dressing for a royal ball.

He hired three people to fashion his gloves: One worked on the palms, another on the fingers, a third on the thumb.

~~~

Clint Eastwood wore the same poncho, without ever washing it, in all three of his "man with no name" westerns.

SURPRISES UNDERNEATH

1. Flamboyant movie star Carmen Miranda refused to wear underwear beneath her outrageous costumes in films of the 1940s.

Her pictures were picketed by ladies' clubs across the nation, even though no one could tell what she was or wasn't wearing under her long dresses.

2. While filming *The Lion in Winter* about the twelfth-century Queen Eleanor of Aquitaine, Katharine Hepburn wore sneakers concealed under her long robes. When asked if that was out of character, Hepburn said that while Eleanor was a queen, she was also "a practical woman who believed in comfort."

3. Isabella, sixteenth-century queen of Spain, vowed not to remove her underwear until her husband captured the Dutch city of Ostend. The Dutch defenders held out for three years.

4. Irish writer James Joyce, whose *Ulysses* is considered one of the greatest books of all time, had an underwear fetish—not for women's panties, for dolls' undies.

In 1814, the Duke of Wellington, England's greatest military hero, was turned away at the door of his club because of his shocking attire. What was he wearing? Trousers.

At that time trousers were considered undignified; gentlemen wore breeches with calf-high silk stockings.

~~~

Tiger infielder Germany Schaefer used clothes to convince an umpire to call a baseball game in 1908.

When it started raining during the game, the ump was unimpressed, until Schaefer took the field wearing raincoat, rubber boots, and rain hat, carrying an umbrella. Game called.

~~~

Before going to bed each night, Hungarian playwright Ferenc Molnár arranged his slippers toe to toe, which he felt created a friendlier sight in the morning than lining them up side by side, which he likened to a married couple not speaking to each other.

~~~

When '60s radical leader Abbie Hoffman appeared on the Merv Griffin TV show, he wore an American-flag shirt.

Network censors objected to his wearing a flag as a piece of clothing and blacked him out of the show. Griffin was left on-screen talking to an apparently invisible man.

~~~

In 1887, Queen Victoria received a bustle with a built-in music box that played the English national anthem, "God Save the Queen," every time she sat down.

ROCK 'N' ROBES

1. In the early days of his singing career (when he knew only three songs), Neil Diamond would take the stage wearing black pants, black shirt, black boots, and a big black cowboy hat, playing a black guitar.

2. When British songwriter/singer Donovan started out, he played in a band called the McCarbs, all of whom dressed in hoods with slits cut out for their eyes.

3. The hot '60s band Paul Revere and the Raiders performed in Revolutionary War uniforms and three-cornered hats. "The outfits gave us a totally unique look," bandleader Mark Lindsay recalled. "Nobody, but nobody was dressing up like idiots."

4. The Beach Boys originally wanted to call their group the Pendletons so they could get free shirts from the Oregon clothing manufacturer.

5. Rock 'n' roll singer Roy Orbison adopted his trademark shades onstage after he accidentally left his regular glasses on a plane. "I was quite embarrassed to go onstage with the shades, but I did it," he recalled.

Stylish basketball star Gary Peyton about fellow million-aire stars Karl Malone and John Stockton: "They don't care what they wear. They wear the too-little jeans, argyle shirts, the old-style shirts with the crocodiles on them. Man."

~~~~

Why did actor Robert Taylor, star of the hit film *Ivanhoe*, want to get out of knight movies? "I'm getting mighty tired of these iron jockstraps," he explained.

~~~~

A clothing manufacturer offered to buy sweatshirt rights from Gene Autry, but the cowboy star told him that he had just been made a better offer. The manufacturer topped the competing offer and Autry accepted.

Then the manufacturer learned that the person he had competed against was one of his own employees calling from another office.

~~~~

Before tennis hustler Bobby Riggs hit the big time by chal-lenging women stars to a battle of the sexes, he would play gimmick tennis matches in an overcoat.

~~~~

Did she, didn't she? When Vassar was a women's college and Jane Fonda a student there, she refused to wear the white gloves and pearls that were required attire for the daily tea in the Rose Parlor.

When told to dress properly, Fonda returned to the parlor wearing the gloves and the pearls—and nothing else.

This story is probably the college equivalent of an urban legend, but one can dream.

HAT'S ALL, FOLKS

1. A mighty clash of egos marked production of the western *The Magnificent Seven*.

Yul Brynner became so convinced that costar Steve McQueen was stealing scenes by manipulating his cowboy hat while other actors (notably Yul) were delivering their lines that he hired an extra to watch McQueen's hat and report all suspicious moves.

2. When Katharine Hepburn made *On Golden Pond* with Henry Fonda, she gave him a hat to wear that once belonged to the love of her life, Spencer Tracy.

3. Writer and actor Robert Benchley wrote and appeared in a magazine ad in the 1930s for the Stetson "3-way hat."

What was a 3-way hat? You could wear the brim down all around, up all around, or as a snap brim. (This may go a long way toward explaining the subsequent unpopularity of hats.)

Benchley dryly concluded that he would rather wear the clever hat box the hat came in than the hat itself.

4. When Mercedes McCambridge made the western movie *Giant*, Gary Cooper lent her one of his old cowboy hats, explaining that it had been properly broken in by being "peed on a lot" by horses.

Cooper was big on sharing his hats. When John Wayne made *True Grit*, his silver hatband was one of Coop's.

4. Writer P. J. O'Rourke: "A hat should be taken off when you greet a lady and left off for the rest of your life. Nothing looks more stupid than a hat."

CHAPTER 14

Marilyn Monroe's toe and other famous body parts

The stars get physical

Most movie stars have body-alike extras who act as their stand-ins during lighting and blocking setups, before the filming starts.

But when Boris Karloff played the monster in *Frankenstein,* they didn't use an extra as his stand-in. They used an iron girder.

When the famous get physical, they're not just any body. Read on:

~~~

When movie star Marilyn Monroe met playwright Arthur Miller, he held her toe and they gazed into each other's eyes. She married him anyway.

~~~

In war, writer and scientist Johann Wolfgang von Goethe proved himself cool under fire. So cool that during a battle he conducted a scientific experiment, charting his own pulse to see how his heart reacted under pressure.

BANGED-UP STARS

Stars have taken their lumps just like you and me. Well, not exactly like the rest of us: They never ring for a nurse and no one shows up.

Fame can lead to greater risk of injury because you try things you wouldn't if you weren't always showing off or putting your famous body on the line.

1. To create the menacing giant of the monster in the original movie *Frankenstein*, star Boris Karloff wore twelve-pound elevated boots and steel bars inside his trousers.

The makeup took four hours each day to be layered on. The bolts on his head left him with scars, and the stress of carrying the weighted costume forced a back operation.

2. Harrison Ford lost two teeth when he fell on a gun during a stunt for a TV show early in his career.

3. Ron Hunt, who became a baseball legend with the early, awful New York Mets, used his body to set dubious baseball records: the single season record for being hit by pitches (50) and the career mark (243).

4. Buster Keaton, who would become one of the most daring of physical comedians, tumbled down a flight of stairs when he was only six months old but was unharmed.

As a toddler, he was part of his family's dangerous vaudeville act. As the Three Keatons demonstrated how to discipline a child, for laughs his father and mother threw baby Buster all over the stage.

5. Jackie Chan made his name in Hong Kong movies by performing his own stunts. Paid the price too: Broke his nose three times, ankle once, most of his fingers, both cheekbones, and his skull.

6. While playing in the musical *Two by Two*, comedian Danny Kaye broke his leg. Didn't put him out of the show, however. Since he had no understudy, Kaye played the role of Noah in a wheelchair.

7. For ring sequences in the boxing movie *Champion*, star Kirk Douglas was filmed going against a number of real boxers to gain an authentic look. They were a little too authentic for Douglas, who was knocked out by one of the boxers who couldn't learn to pull his punches.

Dancer Cyd Charisse was taller than costar Fred Astaire, so to accommodate him she played their close-ups together slumping down on bent knees to make him look taller.

From *Playboy* publisher Hugh Hefner: "We've never retouched our pictures as much as *Vogue, Harper's Bazaar,* and the other women's magazines." Maybe, but they only buy *Cosmo* for the articles.

Busby Berkeley's films always had two things: amazing musical production numbers and gorgeous chorus girls.

The director dressed his chorines in revealing costumes daring for the 1930s—high on the hip, low on the bosom. But one thing Berkeley chorus girls never revealed: their navels. Busby made them all wear navel patches.

When sultry Marlene Dietrich agreed to star in *The Blue Angel,* director Josef von Sternberg didn't like the slight bend in her nose. He had her nose straightened without the help of a plastic surgeon because he wasn't concerned with her real nose, just her on-camera nose.

To make her nose appear straight, he drew a silver line down the middle of her nose. The camera was fooled and so was the audience, many of whom had bent noses of their own.

Lily Tomlin gave away locks of her hair as a bonus for buyers of her home-video library in 1993.

Remember that great scene in the movie *M*A*S*H*, where the doctors play a prank on Hot Lips Houlihan by pulling down the tent while the prudish nurse is taking a shower?

Actress Sally Kellerman didn't want to do the nude shower scene. Made her very nervous. So director Robert Altman prepared a surprise for Kellerman. When the tent was pulled down, there behind the camera stood the entire cast of the movie, stark naked.

Now you know how genuine was that look of shock on Kellerman's face.

~~~

William Howard Taft was the second president to own a car. But he couldn't drive his car because he was too fat to fit behind the wheel.

~~~

Bing Crosby's large ears were pinned back during his early films. Then in the movie *She Loves Me Not,* he went natural—earwise, that is.

~~~

From the ears to the nose, with this observation on the inches of history from French mathematician Blaise Pascal: "Had Cleopatra's nose been shorter, the whole face of the world would have changed."

~~~

Completing the facial tour, at the beginning of his career soul singer Ben E. King was so nervous he had to take lessons from a professional in how to keep his eyes open when he sang onstage.

THEY ALSO HURT THE ONES THEY LOVE

Stars marry stars. They divorce stars. They break their noses.

1. To prepare to play boxer Jake LaMotta in the biopic *Raging Bull,* actor Robert De Niro trained in the ring with the real-life LaMotta, who taught his pupil so well during sparring sessions that an aging LaMotta ended up with black eyes, broken teeth, and a serious chin injury.

During the filming itself, De Niro cracked two of costar Joe Pesci's ribs.

2. In some kind of turnaround being unfair play, Bill Murray broke Robert De Niro's nose during the filming of *Mad Dog and Glory.*

3. In making *Gilda,* Rita Hayworth hit costar Glenn Ford so hard that she knocked out two of his teeth.

When comic actress Judy Holliday met a Hollywood producer to discuss a role, he was too familiar with his hands. Holliday reached into her dress and pulled out her falsies. "I think this is what you want," she informed the producer.

James Madison was the shortest president of the United States, at five-foot-four. We will probably never have a shorter president because of the emphasis put on height in our society and the importance of image over substance to get a politician elected.

～～

In 1908, Broadway producer Oscar Hammerstein enhanced his theatrical income by hiring a performer named Sober Sue to entertain during the play's intermission.

Sober Sue's entire act consisted of standing onstage while people competed for a $1,000 prize if they could make her laugh. Comedians came from all over New York to ply Sue with their best material. None won the prize.

What they didn't know: Her face was paralyzed; she couldn't laugh. But Hammerstein delivered plenty of great comedy to his audiences, and without paying for it.

～～

Many great pool sharks are masters of the cue. But in 1920, billiards wizard Henry Lewis sank forty-six balls in a row using his nose instead of a cue stick.

～～

For some reason, writer Mark Twain attracted a great number of letters from men who claimed to be his double and sent him photographs to prove it.

Twain would reply, congratulating them because "You resemble me more closely than I do myself. I intend to use your picture to shave by."

CELEBRITY DISABILITIES

Actor Rob Lowe: deaf in his right ear.

X-Files star David Duchovny: blind in his right eye due to a basketball injury.

Paul Newman: color-blind.

Nicolas Cage: suffers from vertigo.

Cher: dyslexic.

So was Tom Cruise, although he claimed that Scientology cured him.

Actor Herbert Marshall: had a wooden leg.

Comic actor Dudley Moore: had a club foot that was corrected by surgery.

Singer Johnnie Ray: nearly deaf. Even with a hearing aid, he had trouble hearing the bass and keeping in tempo.

Tamerlane, the Tartar who conquered everything from India to Russia in the fourteenth century, was partially paralyzed. His name actually meant Timur the Lame.

Star Tori Spelling sees her butt as the key to her self-confidence. "I'm really proud of my butt," she said. "I love all my G-strings. They're just so comfortable."

Fred Astaire would disguise his very large hands by curling his middle two fingers while dancing.

CELEBRITY TATTOOS

Just a small sampling of the famous who view their bodies not just as works of art but as the canvas:

1. Next time you see pop singer Ricky Martin, check out the small tattoo of a rose surrounding a heart with an arrow through it. You might have a little trouble spotting it as it's in a semiprivate spot.

2. *Ally McBeal* costar Portia de Rossi has a tattoo of a ring on her right middle finger.

3. Drew Barrymore has three butterfly tattoos.

4. TV actress Alyssa Milano has five tattoos: a heart, fairy, angel, flower, and rosary beads.

5. TV soap actor Peter Reckell has a dagger on his shoulder.

6. Actress Stephanie Seymour has a ring of flowers.

7. Mickey Rourke has at least seven tattoos, including a tiger head with Chinese symbols on his left shoulder, a bull's skull on his right biceps, and the IRA symbol on his left forearm.

8. Sean Connery has two small tattoos on his right arm. One says "Scotland forever," the other "Mum and Dad." He got them when he enlisted in the British navy at the age of sixteen.

At the beach, writer F. Scott Fitzgerald would bury his feet in the sand so strangers couldn't look at them.

Matador Sidney Franklin claimed that writer Ernest Hemingway had a penis no bigger than "a 30-30 shell."

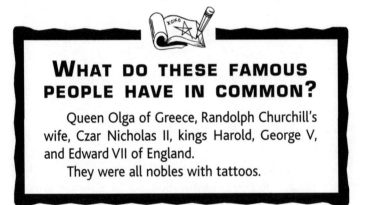

WHAT DO THESE FAMOUS PEOPLE HAVE IN COMMON?

Queen Olga of Greece, Randolph Churchill's wife, Czar Nicholas II, kings Harold, George V, and Edward VII of England.

They were all nobles with tattoos.

CHAPTER 15

What Bob Dylan and Ethel Merman have in common

Odd coincidences among the famous

Trigger? That was Roy Rogers's horse. Well, yes. But not at first.

Before the cowboy star rode Trigger into the pop history books, the palomino belonged to another famous rider: Olivia de Havilland in *The Adventures of Robin Hood.*

That's only one of the many odd little coincidences that crop up in the star-crossed lives of stars.

~

In 1963, Stan "The Man" Musial retired from the St. Louis Cards with an amazing record of equality that will be tough to equal.

Over his long baseball career, he amassed 1,815 hits in home games and 1,815 hits in road games.

Sir George Murray, a nineteenth-century British military hero, was fighting the French in Egypt in 1801 when his men ran out of water in the desert.

Because of his classical education, Murray knew that Julius Caesar had encountered the same problem in the exact same location and solved it by digging through those sands deep enough to find water.

Murray had his men dig to the same depths as Caesar's men, and they found the same spring of water and survived. And now you know the value of a good education.

Judy Garland had a bizarre case of romantic déjà vu:

She starred with the two greatest dancers in film: Gene Kelly in *For Me and My Gal*, then Fred Astaire in *Easter Parade*.

In both movies, the men ask Judy the identical question "Why didn't you tell me I was in love with you?"

WHAT DO THESE FAMOUS PEOPLE HAVE IN COMMON?

Actors Lon Chaney, Wallace Beery, Hans Conried, Toshiro Mifune, Ali MacGraw, Jane Powell, and Debbie Reynolds; baseball pitcher Phil Niekro; playwright Edmond Rostand; and business tycoon Eli Lilly.

They were all born on April Fool's Day.

To outfit the Wizard in the movie version of *The Wizard of Oz*, the studio's wardrobe crew bought some old, elegant-looking coats they found at a secondhand store in L.A.

During filming, actor Frank Morgan (who played the Wizard) found a note inside the pocket of the coat chosen for him. The note was from author L. Frank Baum, who wrote the book upon which the movie was based.

Stunned producers researched and found that the coat, which had been chosen for the Wizard at random, had actually belonged to the real-life wizard who created Oz.

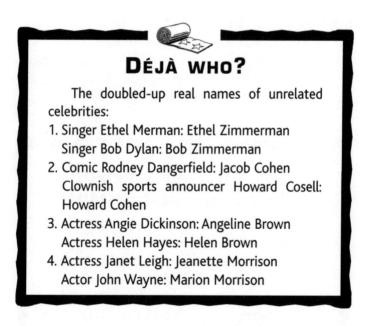

DÉJÀ WHO?

The doubled-up real names of unrelated celebrities:

1. Singer Ethel Merman: Ethel Zimmerman
   Singer Bob Dylan: Bob Zimmerman
2. Comic Rodney Dangerfield: Jacob Cohen
   Clownish sports announcer Howard Cosell: Howard Cohen
3. Actress Angie Dickinson: Angeline Brown
   Actress Helen Hayes: Helen Brown
4. Actress Janet Leigh: Jeanette Morrison
   Actor John Wayne: Marion Morrison

Composer Benjamin Britten was born on St. Cecilia's Day. St. Cecilia is the patron saint of music.

~~~

Motorcycle daredevil Evel Knievel had a cousin who was the exact opposite, we hope: He worked for the Federal Highway Traffic Safety Administration.

~~~

Tom Seaver was one of baseball's greatest pitchers, but he never pitched a no-hitter. He did come very close twice, and twice lost them in the same way.

The first time was in 1969, when in the ninth inning he was one out away from pitching a perfect game when pinch hitter Jim Qualls ruined it with a double.

Six years later, Seaver's bid for a no-hitter also went two outs into the ninth, when Joe Wallis singled.

The team that ruined it both times: the Chicago Cubs.

~~~

A nurse in a hospital in 1977 was reading Agatha Christie's murder mystery *The Pale Horse* when she realized that the hospital's mystery patient had the same symptoms of thallium poisoning as did a victim in the book.

The nurse and Agatha Christie saved the young girl's life.

~~~

The 1959 romantic-comedy *Pillow Talk* was made at the height of Rock Hudson's popularity, when fans didn't know he was secretly gay. In the movie Hudson stars as a heterosexual playboy who pretends to be gay.

FATALLY FAMOUS COINCIDENCES

Even though we all share a common destiny, famous people often receive a special touch from death.

1. William Shakespeare died on his own birthday, his fifty-fifth.

2. The day Judy Garland died, there was a tornado in Kansas.

3. Composer Arnold Schoenberg had an obsessive superstition about the number thirteen. He was convinced he would die at the age of seventy-six because the two numbers totaled thirteen.

In fact, he did die at the age of seventy-six on July thirteenth (a Friday) at ll:47 p.m. (thirteen minutes before midnight).

4. Our second president and our third, John Adams and Thomas Jefferson, died on the same day: July 4, 1826, the fiftieth anniversary of the signing of the Declaration of Independence.

Adams's last words: "Thomas Jefferson lives."

The bizarre coincidence did not so much shock the nation as give it a sense of awe and national destiny.

5. Betty Grable's ex-husband Harry James died on what would have been their fortieth anniversary.

6. Mark Twain was born in November 1835 at the unusual sighting of Halley's Comet. During his life, Twain often suggested that he and the comet were "unaccountable freaks" who came in together and would go out together.

When Twain died in April 1910, Halley's Comet had returned to the skies over Earth.

7. In the comedy *To Be or Not to Be,* actress Carole Lombard asks her costar: "What can happen in a plane?"

The line was edited out before the movie was released to theaters. Why? By then Lombard had died in a plane crash.

8. Just as *Macbeth* is the play stage actors are most superstitious about, *Rebel Without a Cause* is considered a haunted movie.

Four of the movie's stars died young: James Dean in a car crash the same year the film came out. Nick Adams overdosed on drugs in 1968. Sal Mineo was murdered in 1976. Natalie Wood drowned in 1981.

When John Steinbeck's novel *The Wayward Bus* was published, the first edition was being shipped from the printers when the truck carrying the books was struck by a wayward bus traveling on the wrong side of the road.

~~~

Bruce Willis has made six movies with numbers in the title: *The First Deadly Sin, Twelve Monkeys, Four Rooms, The Fifth Element, The Sixth Sense,* and *The Whole Nine Yards.*

~~~

Actor Kevin Kline has played presidents and their impersonating doubles twice to date: He played Dave and President Bob Mitchell in *Dave* and Artemus Gordon and President Ulysses S. Grant in *Wild Wild West.*

~~~

Jamie Lee Curtis starred in the cult horror film *Halloween*. Her mother had a starring role in her own horror classic—Janet Leigh in *Psycho*.

CHAPTER 16

In the realm of the favored spirits

Psychic connections of famous people

Are the famous more psychic, as well as richer and better looking, than the rest of us? Or does it just seem that way?

To achieve fame you need luck, and throwing yourself open to serendipity may create a psychic magnetism.

～～～

At dinner, Julius Caesar and friends discussed the best kind of death. Caesar's opinion: "A sudden one."

The next day was the ides of March, when Caesar was assassinated.

Caesar's sudden death was predicted by a psychic named Spurinna, who forecast danger on the ides of March.

On his way to the senate that day, Caesar saw Spurinna and laughed at the prediction, saying, "The ides of March have come."

"True, they have come," Spurinna replied, "but have not yet gone."

In the fifteenth century a fortune-teller predicted that King Henry IV of England would die in Jerusalem. But Henry never went on a crusade to the Holy Land.

Several years after the prediction, the king was in England's Westminster Abbey when he collapsed from a stroke. He was taken to the abbot's house, where he died.

The name of the room in which he died: the Jerusalem Chamber.

~~~

Race car driver Dale Earnhardt, a year before he died in a race crash, was asked what fellow driver Jeff Gordon had that he did not have?

"A lot of years left to race," Earnhardt replied.

~~~

When Ray Kroc was four years old, his parents took him to a phrenologist, who read the bumps on the boy's head and made this prediction: Ray would work in a restaurant when he grew up.

When Ray Kroc grew up, he founded McDonald's.

~~~

Seventy years before rocket ships were invented, Jules Verne wrote a story about a rocket trip to the Moon, choosing Cape Canaveral as his fictional launch site.

The U.S. Defense Department made the same choice in the 1960s for its secret rocket program because that part of Florida was so remote.

As Constantine led his army toward a fateful battle against Maxentius to determine which general would become emperor of Rome, he had a vision of a flaming cross and the words "In this sign you shall conquer."

A voice instructed him to have his troops inscribe the mark for Christ upon their shields.

Constantine obeyed the vision, won the battle, and became emperor of all Rome, the first emperor to convert to Christianity.

WHAT DO THESE FAMOUS PEOPLE HAVE IN COMMON?

Presidents Ulysses S. Grant, James Garfield, and John Tyler; Queen Victoria; poet Walt Whitman; philosopher Karl Marx; and writers Honoré de Balzac, George Eliot, and Charles-Pierre Baudelaire.

They all believed in the bumpy skull-reading science of phrenology.

When he was twelve, Muhammad Ali drew a picture of a boxing jacket with the words "World Champion" on the back.

〜〜

Before William Blake became famous as a poet and artist, his father tried to apprentice the boy to an engraver. But William, then fourteen, refused to work for engraver William Ryland, declaring, "I do not like the man's face. He looks as if he will live to be hanged."

Young Blake then went to work for another engraver. As for Ryland, he committed forgery several years later and was hanged.

〜〜

Before he joined the Oakland A's, young pitcher Barry Zito turned down two lesser offers to turn pro, then finally signed with the A's for a $1 million bonus.

When he was eight years old, Barry had a school assignment to draw a picture of what he wanted to do in his life. The boy drew a picture of a pitcher below the words: "Making a million dollars."

WHO PUT THE ESP IN ESPN?

All athletes are superstitious, knowing that talent can always use a touch of luck. Players will do the oddest things to manipulate outrageous fortune.

1. Hockey great Wayne Gretzky had a few superstitions during his playing days: When he warmed up, he always shot his first puck wide left. Before each game, he drank a Diet Coke, water, Gatorade, another Diet Coke, and more Gatorade, then ate four hot dogs.

2. Every time Willie Mays went out to play center field, he stepped on second base first.

3. Babe Ruth knocked the dirt out of his spikes after every pitch, even if there was no dirt in his spikes.

4. Sherm Lollar packed his locker with four-leaf clovers.

5. Shortstop Marty Marion picked up imaginary pebbles to prevent the ball from taking bad hops.

6. Hal Chase, Eddie Collins, and Phil Rizzuto all took the gum out of their mouths and stuck it to the button on top of their baseball caps before they stepped in to hit.

7. My favorite baseball superstition: To break out of hitting slumps, Minnie Minoso took a shower in his full uniform and spikes.

8. Then there's the story of Vic Faust, the greatest good-luck charm of all time.

In 1911, Faust told New York Giants manager John McGraw that a fortune-teller had predicted that if Faust pitched for the Giants, they would win the pennant.

One problem: Faust wasn't a pitcher, or even a baseball player.

But the superstitious manager gave him a tryout. Even though Faust was a terrible pitcher, McGraw signed him for the team.

"I'm not superstitious," the manager insisted. "I just don't want anything unlucky to happen."

The Giants won the pennant with Faust riding the bench. When they had the race locked up, McGraw even let him pitch in two games.

McGraw kept Faust on the team for two more years, and the Giants won two more pennants.

The story has a sad but baseball kind of ending: As the fourth season began, Faust didn't show up for spring training. He had been committed to a mental institution. The Giants lost the pennant.

When a judge who had sentenced Father Divine to prison died of a heart attack, the evangelist claimed he caused the judge's death psychically from his jail cell. "I hated to do it," he said.

~~~

When the Treaty of Versailles was signed, ending World War I, French general Ferdinand Foch predicted, "This is not a peace treaty, it is an armistice for twenty years."

That treaty was signed in 1919. Twenty years later, Europe was sunk in World War II.

~~~

When he proposed marriage to poet Elizabeth Barrett, poet Robert Browning picked a book at random from a library and asked the book to predict the future of their love.

The book turned out to be an Italian grammar text, not particularly promising.

Browning opened the book without looking and chanced upon a sentence used as a translation exercise: "If we love in the other world as we do in this," the sentence read, "I shall love thee to eternity."

Not only did his wife love him, she wrote her immortal poems *Sonnets from the Portuguese* for him.

~~~

When the Buddha was five days old, eight Indian psychics predicted that marks on the baby's body meant he was destined to become a great spiritual leader.

Stumbling was considered a bad omen in many countries. So when Napoleon's horse stumbled as he led his army toward Russia, many of his soldiers thought they should turn back.

Napoleon pressed on. His soldiers were right; so was his horse.

~~~

Ronald Knox was a priest and scholar who became chaplain at Oxford. But when Ronald was only four years old, he suffered from insomnia. He was asked how he dealt with sleeplessness at such a young age, and the little boy explained, "I lie awake and think about the past."

~~~

The Romantic poet Percy Bysshe Shelley could not swim, which did not stop him from acting upon a whimsy that he would like to swim. Watching his friends swim in a deep pool, he dove in himself and nearly drowned before a friend pulled him to safety.

Shelley declared with some regret, "I always find the bottom of the well, and they say truth lies there. In another minute I should have found it, and you would have found an empty shell."

Within a few months, Shelley found the bottom, drowning while sailing in foul weather.

Shelley's wife, Harriet, had also died drowning.

British poet Thomas Chatterton, who passed his greatest poems off as the work of another writer, fell by accident into a freshly dug grave.

Gloomily, Chatterton confessed, "I have been at war with the grave for some time and find it not so easy to vanquish. We can find an asylum to hide from every creditor but that."

The next grave was his. The poet killed himself three days later.

CHAPTER 17

Hello, Monica, guess who's running for president?

When star paths cross

They were in two different worlds, but the heavens are strange; they're known to arrange for stars to collide.

⁓

While studying theater at Pasadena Playhouse, Gene Hackman and a classmate were voted Least Likely to Succeed. The classmate was Dustin Hoffman.

⁓

When researching her title role in the biopic about movie star Dorothy Dandridge, movie star Halle Berry discovered that she and Dorothy had been born in the same Cleveland hospital.

⁓

After he lost the presidential election to Bill Clinton, Bob Dole moved into the infamous Watergate apartments. Who lived in the apartment next door? Monica Lewinsky, the intern who nearly brought down the president single-handedly.

General Winfield Scott built up the U.S. Army during the years before the Civil War. He taught strategy and tactics to two young officers who would become the greatest leaders of the coming Civil War—but on opposite sides: Ulysses S. Grant and Robert E. Lee.

Both junior officers served with Scott during the Mexican War in 1846, where they honed their military skills under his direction, as did a hundred other officers who became important leaders for both sides in the war that would decimate a nation.

~~~

Rock Hudson attended the same school as Ann-Margret and Charlton Heston in Winnetka, Illinois.

~~~

When Chevy Chase was in college, before he became famous as one of the original cast members of *Saturday Night Live,* he sometimes sat in with a local band called the Leather Canary.

Two other guys in the band: Walter Becker and Donald Fagen, who went on to become famous as Steely Dan.

~~~

Barbra Streisand and Neil Diamond had a smash hit in 1978 with "You Don't Bring Me Flowers." It was not the first time that the Brooklyn-born superstars had sung together. While students at New York City's Erasmus High School, they both sang in the school choir.

APRIL IS FOR ACTORS

If you want to become a famous actor, get yourself born in April. Here's a partial list of the stars who did:

Marlon Brando and Doris Day (April 3)

Emma Thompson (April 15)

Ellen Barkin, Martin Lawrence, and Jon Cryer (April 16)

James Woods, Rick Moranis, Eric Roberts, Conan O'Brien, Jane Leeves *(Frasier)*, Eric McCormack *(Will & Grace)*, Melissa Joan Hart *(Sabrina the Teenage Witch)* (April 18)

Hugh O'Brian, Don Adams *(Get Smart)*, Dudley Moore, Tim Curry, Ashley Judd, Kate Hudson (April 19)

Jessica Lange, Ryan O'Neal, Denis Leary, Carmen Electra (April 20)

Andie MacDowell, Anthony Quinn, Charles Grodin, Tony Danza (April 21)

Michelle Pfeiffer, Jerry Seinfeld, Daniel Day-Lewis, Uma Thurman (April 29)

Cloris Leachman, Jill Clayburgh, Kirsten Dunst (April 30)

When rock singer David Bowie was a teen, his art teacher was rock singer Peter Frampton's father.

~~~

Before the Civil War, Robert E. Lee served as superintendent of West Point, where he dismissed a young cadet who had no future in the army—but who did become one of America's greatest artists—James McNeill Whistler.

~~~

Strange writer Guy de Maupassant was walking along the river one day when he noticed a man drowning. When the man was pulled out of the water, he turned out to be the bizarre poet Algernon Swinburne.

ROOMIES

1. While both of them were struggling unknowns—before they became character actors who overcame their unusual looks to emerge as stars—Charles Bronson shared a room with Jack Klugman in a New York City boardinghouse.

2. Danny DeVito and Michael Douglas shared an apartment when they were both starting out.

3. Marlon Brando and Wally Cox (who became TV's Mr. Peepers) roomed together when they were both struggling unknowns.

Maybe there are only three famous actors in Australia, but when eventual Oscar winner Mel Gibson was in college, he roomed with eventual Oscar winner Geoffrey Rush. Later at drama school, Gibson starred with eventual two-time Oscar nominee Judy Davis as Romeo and Juliet.

When blues singer Janis Joplin spotted football quarter-back Joe Namath in a bar, she climbed over a table to get to him, and the two of them disappeared together for four days. Can you think of a more unlikely couple?

When movie star Ava Gardner met *Lord of the Rings* author J. R. R. Tolkien, neither knew why the other was famous.

STARS AND THEIR STARS

Happy, happy birthday, baby, baby.

Celebrities have to be born on some day. But why is it always a day that's already taken?

1. Barbra Streisand and Shirley MacLaine share a birthday (April 24), and because they're good friends they celebrated their joint birthday together for years.

2. John F. Kennedy's mother, Rose, had the same birthday (July 22) as would-be president Bob Dole.

3. Actor Michael Douglas was twenty-five years older to the day than his bride when he married actress Catherine Zeta-Jones. The two of them share a birthday, September 25.

THE BIRTHDAY GAME: MATCH THE STARS

Match one star from Column A with one star from Column B, who share the same birthday.

COLUMN A

Singer Jimmy Buffett

Tonight Show host Jack Paar

Basketball star Hakeem Olajuwon

Writer Norman Mailer

Singer Janis Joplin

Fashion designer Gloria Vanderbilt

Composer Stephen Sondheim

Actress Meryl Streep

COLUMN B

Actress Carol Channing

Race car driver Bobby Unser

Singer Judy Collins

Basketball star Detlef Schrempf

Princess Margaret of England

Actress Lindsay Wagner

Football star Larry Csonka

TV evangelist Pat Robertson

ANSWERS

Jimmy Buffett and Larry Csonka: December 25

Jack Paar and Judy Collins: May 1

Hakeem Olajuwon and Detlef Schrempf: January 21

Norman Mailer and Carol Channing: January 31

Janis Joplin and Princess Margaret: January 19

Gloria Vanderbilt and Bobby Unser: February 20

Stephen Sondheim and Pat Robertson: March 22

Triplets

Now try two triplets by linking three stars who were born on the same day: singer Bob Seger, singer Billy Joel, actor George Clooney, singer Jimmie Dale Gilmore, actress Glenda Jackson, news correspondent Mike Wallace.

ANSWERS

Bob Seger, Jimmie Dale Gilmore, and George Clooney: May 6

Glenda Jackson, Mike Wallace, and Billy Joel: May 9

Quadruplets

You're doing so well, let's try two sets of four famous people born on the same day: actress Katharine Hepburn, actress Tori Spelling, actress Debra Winger, composer Burt Bacharach, singer Janet Jackson, comedian George Carlin, actor Emilio Estevez, actor Pierce Brosnan.

ANSWERS

Katharine Hepburn, Burt Bacharach, George Carlin, Emilio Estevez: May 12

Debra Winger, Pierce Brosnan, Janet Jackson, Tori Spelling: May 16

CHAPTER 18

Robert De Niro wants to know: Are you eating those fries?

What famous people do when they're not busy being famous

Sometimes being famous just isn't enough. So celebrities look for little things to fill in the gaps.

~~~

Benjamin Franklin took time away from his statesmanship and inventions to launch an unusual campaign: to change the English alphabet.

Franklin wanted to abolish these letters: *c, j, q, w, x, y.*

He proposed to substitute six new letters, which he claimed would enable every possible sound to be expressed in a single letter.

Whether he undertook this pursuit while flying a kite in a lightning storm is not known.

~~~

Guitarist Les Paul, who had twenty-eight hit records with his wife, Mary Ford, also invented the solid-body electric guitar, multitrack recording, overdub recording, tape echo, and the eight-track tape recorder.

Rockers who are also painters: Michael Clarke of the Byrds, John Lennon and Ringo Starr of the Beatles, Ron Wood of the Rolling Stones, Jerry Garcia of the Grateful Dead, Mickey Dolenz of the Monkees, Randy Meisner of the Eagles, Peter Lewis of Moby Grape, Joe Terry of Danny & the Juniors.

Ian Anderson, lead singer of Jethro Tull, was a salmon farmer and ran his own fishery.

Callers using Bell Atlantic pay phones often heard James Earl Jones's voice assuring them that "This is Bell Atlantic."

ZaSu Pitts was a candy maker as well as a movie star.

Humphrey Bogart played chess by mail with GIs during WW II.

Actor Michael Caine owns seven restaurants: six in London, one in Miami.

Actor Robert De Niro co-owns several restaurants in New York City. No one complained about the food.

Comic actor John Candy was co-owner of the Toronto Argonauts of the Canadian Football League.

For twenty years, singer Bing Crosby owned 15 percent of the Pittsburgh Pirates baseball team.

Basketball star Malik Rose played third board on his high school chess team and earned all-state honors two years in a row on the tuba. In college Rose graduated with dual degrees in computer systems and education.

When most movie actors portray athletes, they take lessons until they can fake prowess at the sport.

Not Rob Brown, who starred opposite Sean Connery as a high school basketball star with a writing talent in the movie *Finding Forrester*. Brown actually was a high school basketball star.

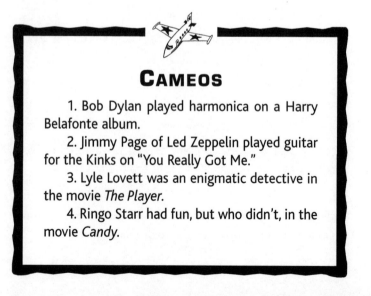

CAMEOS

1. Bob Dylan played harmonica on a Harry Belafonte album.

2. Jimmy Page of Led Zeppelin played guitar for the Kinks on "You Really Got Me."

3. Lyle Lovett was an enigmatic detective in the movie *The Player*.

4. Ringo Starr had fun, but who didn't, in the movie *Candy*.

Welterweight boxing champ Oscar De La Hoya took time out from the ring to cut a CD, for which he was nominated for a Grammy. Didn't win the Grammy, did lose the title.

~~~

Attempting to keep up on world affairs, an average week of reading for historian Friedrich Engels included seven newspapers (in three languages) and nineteen magazines (in eight languages).

~~~

Mary Tyler Moore can belch-talk.

~~~

Martial arts movie star Jean-Claude Van Damme studied ballet.

~~~

Presidential candidate Barry Goldwater taught himself to play "Silent Night" on the trombone.

~~~

In tenth grade, future actress Holly Hunter placed eighth nationally in a poultry-judging contest. Hunter is also so good on the piano, she played the music in the movie *The Piano*.

~~~

Actress Geena Davis was a semifinalist for the United States Olympic archery team in 1999. She's also a member of MENSA.

~~~

Basketball great Tim Duncan collects knives.

Baseball star Mark Grace can name the capital of any state. This is an impressive feat among schoolkids and baseball stars.

Jodie Foster dubs her own voice in the French versions of her movies because she speaks French fluently.

In high school, movie star Richard Gere was a member of the student council. One of those overachieving kids, he was also on the gymnastics, lacrosse, and ski teams and played trumpet in the band.

When baseball great Dave Winfield was in college, he was drafted by pro teams in all three major sports: baseball, football, and basketball.

Meryl Streep was a high school cheerleader and homecoming queen.

Casanova, the legendary Italian lover, was also a hardworking librarian, soldier, doctor, government official, spy, and Greek translator.

Working in so many different fields, how exactly did he find the time to become a legend of love? No television back then.

Finally, we have the unusual case of Ruby the elephant, who was famous in Phoenix for being an elephant, quite an achievement when you consider she lived in a desert where temperatures reach 110 and stay that way for seven months of the year.

But that wasn't enough for Ruby.

Phoenix Zoo keepers noticed that the elephant liked to brush dirt with a tree branch held in her trunk. They gave her paints and a giant brush. Ruby became such a popular artist that her paintings sold for as much as $3,500.

If an elephant can become famous, so can you.

CHAPTER 19

Champagne screams

Love and sex among the elite

Movie star Katharine Hepburn sets the stage for the passion play of love and lust among the illustrious as she ponders: "I often wonder whether men and women really suit each other. Perhaps they should live next door and just visit now and then."

Too late for the turbulence-prone, whose affairs are lovingly detailed below:

~

Miami Dolphins football coach Don Shula, before he proposed to the woman who became his wife, had her do backpedaling drills.

"I wanted to find out about her athletic ability," he explained. "This was going to be a serious relationship, and I wanted my kids to possibly be defensive backs."

~

W. C. Fields, the comic movie star, was so suspicious of his girlfriends that he hired detectives to follow them and see if they were cheating on him. One of them was: She married the detective who was tailing her.

When John Adams became the second president of the young United States, a rumor made the rounds that he had sent a general to England to choose four women as mistresses, two for each of them.

Adams refuted this scandalous rumor, saying, "If this be true, he has kept them all for himself and cheated me out of my two."

Anna Nicole Smith, a Playboy Playmate and stripper, married millionaire oil tycoon J. Howard Marshall II when he was in his eighties and she was in her twenties. She spent years after his death litigating with his sons over a share of the huge family inheritance.

In court testimony, the family lawyer said Marshall had trouble making up his mind whether he should marry Smith or adopt her.

Football legend Paul Hornung, asked why he got married in the morning, replied: "Because if it doesn't work out, I don't want to blow the whole day."

Rock star Chrissie Hynde offered this advice for all wannabe rock singers (all of whom, at last count, ignored it): "Try not to have a sexual relationship with the band. It always ends in tears."

WHAT DO THESE FAMOUS PEOPLE HAVE IN COMMON?

Actors Clint Eastwood, Danny Glover, Stuart Whitman, Alicia Silverstone, and Rob Schneider; singers Courtney Love, Tony Martin, and Johnny Mathis.

They were all born in the most romantic city in the United States: San Francisco.

Before Rudolph Valentino became a matinee idol, he married an aspiring actress named Jean Acker. On their wedding night, she ran into the bedroom and bolted the door to keep Valentino out, the opposite instinct of all the American women who would soon come to worship the screen's number one lover.

~~~

Movie star Joan Crawford was married four times, each time for four years. Each time she married a new man, she had new toilet seats installed throughout her mansion.

~~~

When movie star Clara Bow spurned a lover, he tried to commit suicide by slitting his wrists. "He's got to be kidding," she exclaimed. "Men don't slash their wrists. They use a gun."

When a young Marie Curie worked as a governess, she fell in love with the wealthy family's son, but the parents refused to allow them to marry.

Marie contemplated suicide, then got over it and moved on into scientific research, saying, "Life does not deserve to be worried over."

~~~

A censor from the film board objected to a scene of Marilyn Monroe and Yves Montand rolling around on a bed in the movie *Let's Make Love,* explaining that because both actors were horizontal it was too much like making love.

"Oh, that," Marilyn pointed out. "You can do that standing up."

The scene stayed, although the censor was too embarrassed to stick around.

~~~

Sophia Loren said: "Sex appeal is 50 percent what you've got and 50 percent what people think you've got."

~~~

Writer Thomas Wolfe kept a to-do list of women he hadn't slept with but planned to get around to.

Wolfe, who wrote *Look Homeward, Angel,* claimed he had plenty of women to sleep with. "The kind of woman that is really hard for me to find," he complained, "is a typist who can read my writing."

~~~

Which Hollywood star did Joan Crawford say she would become a lesbian for? Greta Garbo.

Dennis Hopper claimed he once tried to have an orgy with actress Natalie Wood, who wanted a champagne bath. After he filled the tub with champagne, she took off her clothes and got in, only to leap out screaming in pain. He took her to the hospital.

On his wedding night, Franklin P. Adams, celebrated newspaper columnist and Algonquin Round Table regular, excused himself from the bridal chamber to play poker with the boys, explaining that he was obligated since they had chipped in for an expensive wedding gift.

In the third century, Roman Emperor Claudius banned marriage because married soldiers didn't fight hard enough. When one priest defied the ban and married couples anyway, the emperor had him beaten to death. The priest's name: Valentine, and that's how we got the lovers' celebration, Valentine's Day.

Goldie Hawn in 1977: "Monogamy is impossible these days for both sexes. I don't know anyone who's faithful or wants to be."

When he ran a movie studio, millionaire Howard Hughes kept five houses in various L.A. neighborhoods and a different mistress installed in each one, giving Hughes a unique solution to those L.A. traffic jams.

As a young but already eccentric painter, Salvador Dali seduced a wealthy American woman. But when she removed her clothes, he did not take her to bed. Instead, Dali fried two eggs, placed them upon her bare shoulders and bade her goodnight.

~~~

Movie stars often have brief flings during the filming of their pictures. But they usually agree that they have.

When Jeremy Irons and Meryl Streep made the passionate romance *The French Lieutenant's Woman,* he claimed they had an intense affair that lasted only through the production, but she said they never did. Only one of them got it right, but which one?

~~~

Lady Caroline Lamb, the Madonna of the 1800s, once surprised her husband on his birthday (he was prime minister of England) by having herself served naked as a banquet dish.

~~~

Actor John Barrymore, one of Hollywood's most notorious drunks, rented a brothel in India for an entire week to service a single customer: himself.

~~~

The philosophy of France's most beloved cabaret singer, Edith Piaf: "You know more about a guy in one night in bed than you do in months of conversation. In the sack, they can't cheat."

Italian poet and painter Dante Rossetti wrote most of his early poems for his wife, Elizabeth Siddal. When she killed herself in 1862, Rossetti buried the poems with her.

Eight years later, he began to think more passionately of his poems than of Elizabeth. He obtained permission to open her grave and removed the poems. He had them published to great success.

~~~

Pablo Picasso on women: "For me there are only two kinds: goddesses and doormats."

~~~

When Alexander the Great conquered Persia, he solidified control by ordering ten thousand of his soldiers to marry Persian women. Alexander married a Persian woman too because, as a good leader, he never asked his soldiers to go where he wouldn't go himself.

~~~

Novelist Sinclair Lewis was determined to marry journalist Dorothy Thompson. In the 1920s he followed her across Europe and into Russia to plead his case. She remained dubious.

At a dinner party, the author was asked to give a speech. Lewis stood, said, "Dorothy, will you marry me?" then sat down.

She eventually said yes. They eventually divorced.

Charlie Chaplin installed a telescope in his L.A. mansion to spy into the bedroom of his movie-star neighbor, John Barrymore.

~~~~~

From playwright George Bernard Shaw, who never saw how booties are shaken today, came this observation about dancing: "A perpendicular expression of a horizontal desire."

~~~~~

Leave it to Woody Allen to point out the obvious advantage of becoming bisexual: "It immediately doubles your chances for a date on Saturday night."

~~~~~

From the wit Dorothy Parker comes this romantic plaint:
Why is it no one ever sent me yet
One perfect limousine, do you suppose?
Ah no, it's always just my luck to get
One perfect rose.

~~~~~

And to end this chapter of quirky love, an actual romantic note:
From the time they met, until his death, Elvis sent a roomful of flowers to Ann-Margret whenever she opened up a show in Las Vegas.

CHAPTER 20

Darling, here's that Komodo dragon I promised you. Won't you take off your shoes and relax?

Animal tales

There is no Hamlet among the lions.

Not much second guessing among mice either.

Animals are pure ego. They act, take the consequences, and make no excuses. Perhaps that's why the famous are attracted to animals: They're jealous.

~

Famed Indian yogi K. N. Udupa trained rats to perform yoga postures.

~

President Andrew Johnson kept pet mice in the White House. Historians have overlooked the president's position on rodent-yoga.

~

Dictator Idi Amin inducted Ugandan military heroes into the Order of the Mosquito. Amin chose the mosquito as his symbol of victory to honor the pest for keeping European settlers out of Uganda.

In 1814, Chilean revolutionaries tried to overthrow the Spanish imperialists. The rebels were losing a critical battle when their leader, Bernardo O'Higgins, devised a unique strategy.

O'Higgins had his soldiers gather every animal in the village (all the horses, mules, dogs, and pigs) and stampede them toward the Spanish lines.

The Spanish forces were so unnerved by the bizarre animal attack that they broke ranks, and the rebels escaped the trap.

O'Higgins and his men eventually won the war, with their leader becoming the first president of the new country.

~~~

A seventeenth-century Indian emperor, Jahān-gīr, invented a unique form of fishing. Whenever he caught a fish, he would string pearls through the fish's gills and toss it back in the water.

~~~

During a movie production, Jack Nicholson was thrown from his horse and broke his wrist. But he climbed back up on the horse and finished shooting the scene.

What's significant is his explanation: "I was scared. I wouldn't have gotten back on the horse if I were a real person."

That's what separates the famous: They believe their own publicity. Nicholson acts like Nicholson because he knows how Nicholson is supposed to act.

The eccentric painter Salvador Dali took his pet ocelot to a Manhattan restaurant, alarming a woman there.

Dali reassured her that the ocelot was actually a cat "painted over with an op art design."

The woman sighed in relief and admitted, "I can see now what it is," she said. "At first I thought it was a real ocelot."

~~~

Joel Harris, who wrote the beloved Uncle Remus stories, settled into an Atlanta house called Snap Bean Farm in 1881. Harris so loved animals that when he found a bird nesting in his mailbox, he built a new mailbox rather than disturb the bird, and he changed the name of the house to the Wren's Nest.

~~~

In June 2001, movie star Sharon Stone came up with a unique gift for her husband, newspaper editor Phil Bronstein: She arranged for a private tour of the L.A. Zoo.

A zookeeper took Bronstein into a cage to see a Komodo dragon close up, suggesting he remove his white tennis shoes because the dragon was fed white rats and might mistake his shoes for rats.

When Bronstein took off his shoes, the seven-foot Komodo dragon attacked, bit his foot, and crushed his big toe.

Happy birthday, Phil. You sure you don't want to watch *Basic Instinct* one more time before you go home?

Mickey Rourke walked off the set of a film because the producers refused to cast his pet chihuahua in the movie.

Roman Emperor Heliogabalus was a practical joker with the power to stage elaborate jokes. He once threw a feast, making sure his friends got so drunk they passed out. His servants then carried them into an arena.

When they woke up, the emperor's pals were surrounded by lions, leopards, and bears. The animals were all de-fanged and de-toothed, but it took the victims a while to figure that out.

WHAT DO THESE FAMOUS PEOPLE HAVE IN COMMON?

Singers Fabian, Frankie Avalon, Bobby Rydell, Chubby Checker, Joan Jett, Patti LaBelle; actors Will Smith, Kevin Bacon, Peter Boyle, Imogene Coca, Richard Gere; comedians Bill Cosby and David Brenner.

They were all born in Philly.

When notorious boxer Stanley Ketchel had the theory of evolution explained to him, he spent the day staring at a bowl of goldfish, then pronounced evolution to be false.

"I've been watching those fish for hours," he explained, "and they haven't changed one bit."

~~~

Football star Bronko Nagurski was such a powerful running back that he once barreled through the end zone and knocked over a policeman. The policeman happened to be on top of a horse when Nagurski hit him. Knocked over the horse too.

~~~

Paul McCartney was always thinking of his fans, even fans people didn't realize the Beatles had.

When the group recorded "A Day in the Life," McCartney added an ultrasonic whistle that only dogs could hear. He did it for his own English sheepdog, Martha, and all the other dogs out there who believed in Beatlemania.

~~~

Animals inspired artist Pablo Picasso to offer this challenging view of the Almighty Creator: "God is really only another artist. He invented the giraffe, the elephant, and the cat. He has no real style. He just goes on trying other things."

CHAPTER 21

May the Force teach you how to drive

Stars in cars, watch out

We all know they should never let famous people drive. They all get arrested for speeding or drunk driving or, in the case of O. J. Simpson, slow driving.

So when they say "Want to go for a drive?" you say, "I'll walk."

~~~

Baseball slugger José Canseco bought his wife a BMW but preferred a Porsche for himself. He showed why when the couple had a fight and she drove off in her BMW. He raced after her in his Porsche and rammed her car with his. Canseco was used to hitting things that go ninety miles per hour.

~~~

In his early twenties, George Lucas was in a bad car crash and spent months in the hospital. While recuperating, he gave up the idea of becoming a race car driver and created the concept of the Force.

Jan (of Jan and Dean) crashed his car while speeding, which sent him into a long coma, ending the duo's rock 'n' roll career.

Only weeks before the crash, Jan was speeding at one hundred miles per hour in a T-Bird for fifteen miles before the cops could catch him. Jan got out of an arrest that might have turned his life around by giving the cops autographed albums for their kids.

~~~

A month after he was arrested for impersonating a police officer to intimidate the other people in a car accident, Olden Polynice, seven-foot center for the NBA's Utah Jazz, was charged with doing it all over again: He cut off a couple in traffic, then flashed a badge and claimed to be with the California Sheriff's Office.

The L.A. Police Department had given Polynice an honorary badge, but the badge gave him no authority.

~~~

In 1971, Grace Slick of Jefferson Airplane smashed her Mercedes into a wall near the Golden Gate Bridge, forcing the cancellation of a recording session and nearly of her life.

~~~

In 1976, Keith Richards of the Rolling Stones fell asleep at the wheel and crashed his car north of London.

~~~

Bonnie and Clyde, who were turned into legendary outlaw stars after their deaths, were killed in their car, shot 187 times by lawmen tired of their speeding away.

Burt Reynolds played college football and was good enough to be drafted by the Baltimore Colts. But he gave up the gridiron for acting after damaging both knees in a car accident.

~~~

Rock 'n' roller Eddie Cochran, who might have become the next Elvis, was killed in a taxi crash in London in 1960. Cochran's song on the charts at the time: "Three Steps to Heaven."

~~~

Keith Moon, drummer for the Who, had a different kind of hobby: He liked to drive expensive cars into swimming pools to watch them sink.

~~~

Blonde bombshell Jayne Mansfield, being groomed to become the next Marilyn Monroe, died in a car crash when she was thirty-five.

~~~

Wild artist Jackson Pollock committed suicide by car when he was forty-four.

~~~

Wild dancer Isadora Duncan, who lost both her children in a car crash, broke her neck when her long, flowing scarf was caught by a wheel of the car she was driving.

~~~

Actress Grace Kelly, princess of Monaco, had a stroke at the wheel and drove her car off a cliff.

CHAPTER 22

Pigeons flee Ernest Hemingway

Movable celebrity feasts

If you are what you eat, the famous must be dining at a different table from the rest of us. Let's chow down with them and find out.

～～

Elvis once flew a thousand miles with all his hangers-on to get a peanut butter and jelly sandwich. Not just any PB&J but a sandwich fit for a King.

～～

After finishing a cup of tea on a movie set, Alfred Hitchcock would toss the cup over his shoulder. The smash of cup on floor was an object lesson to his cast and crew, demonstrating who had the clout to act outrageously on a Hitchcock set.

～～

Because Paul Cézanne was such a slow painter, he used wax fruit as models for his still lifes. Real fruit would rot before he finished painting a picture.

The great American singer Josephine Baker lived in Paris during the Nazi occupation and joined the French Resistance fighters.

Suspecting that she was a conspirator, a Nazi officer poisoned the singer. He put cyanide in Baker's dinner, then ordered her to eat the fish at gunpoint.

Even so, Baker managed to reach Resistance comrades. A doctor pumped her stomach and she survived, although she lost all her hair from the cyanide and wore a wig for the rest of her life.

~~~~~

When actress Helen Hayes decided to cook her first Thanksgiving turkey, she told her family that if the bird didn't come out right, they'd all go have dinner at their favorite hotel.

When she carried the turkey from the kitchen into the dining room, she found her entire family sitting at the table in their hats and coats.

~~~~~

Before Fiorello La Guardia became a popular mayor of New York City in 1933, he was a judge. One day he presided over the case of a poor man who had stolen a loaf of bread to feed his family.

La Guardia recognized that by law the man must be fined $10. Then the judge paid the fine himself, adding: "I'm going to fine everyone in this court 50 cents for living in a town where a man has to steal bread in order to eat."

The judge had the bailiff collect the fines and give them to the man.

General Ulysses S. Grant's regular breakfast: a cucumber soaked in vinegar.

That's the breakfast of a man who is going to win the battle no matter what it takes, which was Grant's approach to leading Union troops in the Civil War.

~~~

When the great baseball pitcher Rube Waddell signed a contract with the Philadelphia Athletics, he didn't demand more money. Instead, he insisted on a clause preventing his roommate, Ossee Schreckengost, from eating animal crackers in bed.

~~~

Early in his career, Ernest Hemingway was a down-and-out writer living in Paris. He fed his family by wringing the necks of pigeons he trapped in the Luxembourg Gardens, then sneaking them out of the park hidden in his son's baby carriage.

WHAT DO THESE FAMOUS ROCKERS HAVE IN COMMON?

Jan and Dean, Petula Clark, Ray Charles, Roy Orbison, Lesley Gore, Vanilla Fudge, the Bee Gees, Aretha Franklin, the Moody Blues, the Fifth Dimension, and the Supremes.

They all sang the "Things go better with Coke" jingle for Coca-Cola during the '60s.

The eccentric eighteenth-century Lord of the Admiralty, the Earl of Sandwich (yes, the one for whom that luncheon mainstay is named), once threw a lavish dinner for his wealthy friends and had a baboon led in, dressed as a minister, to say grace.

This affront would have caused even more of a sensation if the baboon had actually said grace.

Why was writer Isaac Bashevis Singer a vegetarian? "Out of consideration for the chicken."

Hard-boiled detective writer Mickey Spillane explained why his tough guy hero, Mike Hammer, drank beer in all Spillane's books: "He drinks beer, not cognac, because I can't spell *cognac.*"

Among pudgy pitchers, Mickey Lolich of the Detroit Tigers was one of the best in baseball, and a favorite of couch potatoes across the country. He knew why: "All the fat guys watch me and say to their wives, 'See, there's a fat guy doing okay. Bring me another beer.'"

Nutritionally minded ascetics aren't the only people who think you are what you eat. Here's famed Green Bay Packers receiver Max McGee: "When it's third and ten, you can take the milk drinkers, and I'll take the whiskey drinkers every time."

THOUGHT FOR FOOD

1. Writer Ambrose Bierce: "Edible—Good to eat and wholesome to digest, as a worm to a toad, a toad to a snake, a snake to a pig, a pig to a man, and a man to a worm."

2. Chef James Beard: "A gourmet who thinks of calories is like a tart who looks at her watch."

3. Indian philosopher Mahatma Gandhi: "God comes to the hungry in the form of food."

4. Movie star Robert Redford: "Health food may be good for the conscience, but Oreos taste a hell of a lot better."

5. Irish playwright Brendan Behan: "I have a total irreverence for anything connected with society except that which makes the roads safer, the beer stronger, the food cheaper, and the old men and old women warmer in the winter and happier in the summer."

6. Writer Herman Melville: "If I have done the hardest possible day's work and then come to sit down in a corner and eat my supper comfortably—why, then I don't think I deserve any reward for my hard day's work—for am I not now at peace? Is not my supper good?"

Reggie Jackson was one of baseball's greatest sluggers, but his fielding talents were rocky. When Yankees teammate Graig Nettles heard that Jackson had the "Reggie" bar named in his honor, he questioned the move: "What does he need another candy bar for? He's already got one: Butterfingers."

Beau Brummell, arbiter of fashion for Regency England, declared vegetables unfashionable. Asked by a society matron if he had ever eaten a vegetable, Brummell replied, "Yes, madam, I once ate a pea."

William Jennings Bryan, a frequent candidate for president, drank no alcohol. So he faced a dilemma when asked at an official dinner to toast Japanese Admiral Tōgō, whose strategy had given the Japanese navy a surprise victory in the Russo-Japanese War.

Determined to touch no alcohol, even ceremonial champagne, Bryan solved the problem by raising a glass of water.

"Admiral Tōgō has won a great victory on the water," he announced to the assembly. "I will, therefore, toast him in water. When Admiral Tōgō wins a victory on champagne, I will toast him in champagne."

For her wedding feast, movie star Lana Turner had "I love you" spelled out in pimentos in the sides of baked hams.

The privileges of power: When Lyndon Johnson became president, he had a new tap added to White House sinks—a tap that dispensed Fresca instead of water.

~~~

Writer H. L. Mencken hired a mathematician to calculate how many cocktails could be made from the booze stocked in a complete bar. The answer: 17,864,392,788. How many of them Mencken personally consumed is lost to history.

CHAPTER 23

Baby Greatest and the old guy who pulled ten boats

Celebrity surprises of youth and old age

EARLY STARS

Famous people who could do things at an early age we couldn't do all grown up:

~~~

Actor, singer, and dancer Donald O'Connor made his stage debut at the age of three days, when his vaudevillian father cast him as a baby in the family act, a role Donald played convincingly.

~~~

Boxing champ Muhammad Ali knocked out one of his mother's teeth with a baby punch. He was eighteen months old at the time and already the greatest.

~~~

Writer Thomas Wolfe could read at the age of two.

Young Wolfgang Mozart had an amazing ear for music. When he was only two years old, he heard a pig squeal and said, "G-sharp." There was a piano in the house, and it proved the boy was right.

Princess Anne of England took her first riding lessons when she was two and a half. Twenty years later, she won the European Championships.

Philosopher-to-be John Stuart Mill read in both English and Greek at the age of three.

Shirley Temple took her first dance class at three. By five, she was a movie star, although the studio publicity department, honoring the Hollywood tradition of lying about things they don't have to lie about, told the world that she was four. Apparently, five was over the hill for a child star.

Actress Jodie Foster read by the time she was three years old and at the same age made her acting debut in a Coppertone suntan lotion commercial.

Mystery writer Rex Stout had read the Bible by the time he was three. He read Gibbon's *Decline and Fall of the Roman Empire* at four. At the same age, he could add long columns of six-digit numbers within seconds.

Precocious tennis star Tracy Austin took up the game at three. She made the cover of *World Tennis* magazine a year later.

〜

H. L. Hunt, who became one of the world's richest men, read the financial pages of the daily paper when he was only three years old. He was home-schooled.

〜

Jazz great Quincy Jones grew up in Chicago's tough South Side, where he carried a switch blade at the age of four to protect himself.

〜

Louis XIV, the Sun King, became king of France at four.

〜

Gustav Mahler composed his first music at four.

〜

Kim Ung-Yong, a South Korean genius, could speak fluent Japanese, German, and English by the time he was four.

〜

Fred Astaire landed his first job in show biz at five.

〜

Jazz great Mose Allison discovered at five that he could play the piano by ear.

〜

Wolfgang Mozart began composing music at five.
So did Sergey Prokofiev.

The Dalai Lama ascended to the throne of Tibetan Buddhism when he was five.

~~~

Movie star Charles Bronson claims to have lost his virginity at the age of five to a girl of six. Details remain sketchy.

~~~

At the age of six, Nadia Comaneci entered state-supported gymnastics training in Rumania, practicing up to four hours a day. She became world champion within a decade, and her career was over a few years after that, at about the age everyone else's career is just starting.

~~~

Country singer Dolly Parton wrote her own songs and played them on the mandolin at six.

~~~

By age seven, Orson Welles had memorized *King Lear*. Not just Lear's lines but the entire play.

~~~

Pianist Jose Iturbi taught piano lessons at seven.

~~~

Annie Oakley supported her large family as a markswoman selling the extra game she shot—at nine.

~~~

Dutch inventor Zacharias Janssen designed the first compound microscope when he was only ten years old.

Cardinal Georges d'Amboise, adviser to the king of France, became a bishop when he was fourteen.

~~~~~

The winner of the first Miss America title in Atlantic City in 1921 remains the youngest and shortest beauty to win. Margaret Gorman was only fifteen when she won and stood just five-foot-one.

Because of changes in rules and fashions, we'll probably never have a younger Miss America, or a shorter one.

~~~~~

Alexander the Great led his father's army into battle at the age of sixteen. Won too.

LATE BLOOMERS

Famous people who did remarkable things late in life when most people are calling it quits:

~~~~~

Jazz pianist and composer Eubie Blake performed until his death at one hundred. A heavy smoker and drinker all his life, Blake said when he reached the centennial mark, "If I'd known I was going to live this long, I'd have taken better care of myself."

Painter Grandma Moses began her career in art when she was seventy-eight years old, completing more than one thousand oil paintings.

If she had begun when she was twenty and kept up the pace she would have created enough paintings to fill all the museums in the world.

~~~

When in his seventies, the great Italian painter Titian remarked, "I think I am beginning to learn something about painting."

~~~

Composer Johannes Brahms gave up composing in his old age to enjoy the time left to him. A few months later, he started composing again, announcing, "After a few days away from it, I was so happy at the thought of no more writing that the music came to me without effort."

~~~

Car mogul Henry Ford could do a handstand at the age of seventy-five.

Beauty product mogul Elizabeth Arden could do a head-stand at the age of seventy-five.

Many people at the age of seventy-five can no longer do a foot stand.

~~~

Fitness guru Jack LaLanne was amazing when he was young, more amazing when he was old. At the age of sixty-six, LaLanne swam a mile in the ocean off the Florida coast, pulling behind him seventy-seven people on ten boats.

The great Satchel Paige was the oldest pitcher to play in a major league game, throwing three shutout innings for the Kansas City A's against the Boston Red Sox in 1965 when he was fifty-nine years old. Because of questions about his real age, Paige may have been even older than that.

At the age of fifty-three, the great shortstop Minnie Minoso played for the Chicago White Sox in a few games and went 1-for-8 before retiring.

～～～

When the painter Henri Matisse was in his eighties, he could no longer sit up to paint a canvas. So he attached a brush to a long stick and painted while lying in his bed.

～～～

Circus performer Karl Wallenda walked a tightrope suspended from the top floors of two Miami hotels when he was seventy-two years old. But he died at that age, falling from another high wire.

～～～

Classical pianist Mieczyslaw Horszowski recorded an album at the age of ninety-nine.

～～～

Amos Alonzo Stagg coached the football team at the College of the Pacific when he was eighty-four.

CHAPTER 24

Four hundred thousand beetles can't be wrong

The great egos of great people

Jesus Christ could walk on water, but his curve ball was suspect.

Baseball great Ted Williams evaluated his hitting talents this way: "Jesus H. Christ Himself couldn't get me out."

Welcome to the world of celebrated egos.

~~~

Movie star Joan Crawford hired an assistant to stay on the set of her pictures and whisper compliments into her ear between takes.

~~~

Playwright Eugene O'Neill wrote long plays and refused to make changes. When a director pleaded with him to cut the lengthy *Ah, Wilderness,* O'Neill finally agreed to cut out fifteen minutes—which he did, not by shortening the script but by eliminating one of the intermissions.

When a theater director asked playwright Oscar Wilde to make some changes in his script, Wilde declined, explaining, "Who am I to tamper with a masterpiece?"

~

Renowned engineer Charles Steinmetz was once hired by General Electric to find out what was wrong with one of the company's advanced systems.

Steinmetz studied the equipment, then drew an X in chalk on a particular section of one unit. When the GE technicians took apart the machine, they discovered that Steinmetz had been right. The problem resided in the exact spot under his X.

But GE executives objected to Steinmetz's $10,000 bill for his brief services. Steinmetz explained: "Making one chalk mark: $1. Knowing where to place it: $9,999."

~

Why is February so short of days? Because it suited the vanity of a famous man.

Augustus Caesar took one day out of February and gave it to the month of August. Why? So that the month of July (named after his uncle Julius Caesar) wouldn't be longer than his own name-month.

~

Two philosophers from ancient Greece wrangled over the dilemma of ego:

Through careful and frequent flattery, Aristippus made himself popular in the court of Dionysius, ruler of the city-state of Syracuse. Diogenes remained his own man, living in the not-unfamiliar combination of free thought and poverty.

"If you would only learn to compliment Dionysius," Aristippus pointed out while Diogenes prepared a meager meal of lentils, "you wouldn't have to live on lentils."

As Diogenes stirred the pot, he countered, "If you would only learn to live on lentils, you wouldn't have to flatter Dionysius."

Yet it's Diogenes who became legend, while Aristippus is only remembered as paling next to Diogenes.

～～～

John Foster Dulles, powerful politician and secretary of state, admitted that once in his political career he had made a bad decision.

"I thought I had made a wrong decision," he explained. "But it turned out I had been right."

So how was he wrong?

Dulles confessed: "I was wrong to have thought that I was wrong."

～～～

When scientists observed the curvature of space during a solar eclipse, their experiment validated Albert Einstein's predictions about his theory of relativity.

When Einstein was asked what he would have said if the observations had not confirmed his thinking, he replied, "I would have been obliged to pity our dear God. The theory is correct."

Chicago Mayor Bill Thompson made it illegal to speak English in 1935. He had the state legislature declare that "American" was the official language of Illinois.

~~~

As a young man, French prime minister Georges Clemenceau fought several duels. He went off to face one challenge accompanied by a friend, who was surprised when Clemenceau bought a one-way ticket at the train station. The friend asked Clemenceau if he really felt that pessimistic about his chances in the duel.

"Not at all," Clemenceau responded happily. "I always use my opponent's return ticket for the trip back."

~~~

Basketball great Charles Barkley when he found out he was misquoted in his own autobiography: "I should have read it."

~~~

While passing through St. Peter's Cathedral, the sculptor Michelangelo heard someone misstate that another artist had created his "Pieta."

After they left, Michelangelo chiseled his name on the statue of Mary. It was the only time he signed any of his works.

~~~

Absurdist writer Gertrude Stein once asked a friend: "Besides Shakespeare and me, who do you think there is?"

THE UN-EGO: HUMILITY IS WHERE YOU CAN FIND IT

1. USC football coach John McKay put the game in perspective: "There are still over sixty million Chinese who don't care if we win or lose."

2. When Adlai Stevenson was running for president, he asked a group of kids how many of them would like to be a candidate for president of the United States someday. Many hands shot up.

Then Stevenson said, "How many candidates for president would like to be children again?" One hand went up.

3. While walking to a party being held in his honor, Ulysses S. Grant fell into step with a stranger heading to the same party. This man admitted that while he was going to see the famed general out of curiosity, "I have always thought that Grant was a very much overrated man."

"That's my view also," Grant agreed.

4. After Broadway songwriter Oscar Hammerstein had two big hits (*Oklahoma!* and *Carmen Jones*), he took out an ad in the show biz trade journal *Variety*: "Holiday greetings from Oscar Hammerstein II, author of *Sunny River* (six weeks at the St. James), *Very Warm for May* (seven weeks at the Alvia), *Three Sisters* (seven weeks at the Drury Lane), *Ball at the Savoy* (five weeks at the Drury Lane), *Free for All* (three weeks at the Manhattan). I've done it before and I can do it again!"

In their joint workshop, the two artists James Whistler and Walter Sickert were printing their etchings. When a plate slipped out of Sickert's hands, Whistler shook his head and said in disgust, "How like you."

But when Whistler himself dropped a plate, he exclaimed in surprise, "How unlike me."

～～～

His novel *Main Street* made Sinclair Lewis famous. But not famous enough to impress movie mogul Jack Warner.

When Warner's studio bought movie rights to the book, the boss changed the title to *I Married a Doctor,* under the theory that no one wanted to see "a picture about a street."

Lewis had the last laugh, sort of: The movie flopped.

～～～

Media mogul Ted Turner also dabbled in sports, owning the Atlanta Braves, Atlanta Hawks, and Jane Fonda. Turner believed in facing up to his own faults: "If I only had a little humility," he explained, "I would be perfect."

～～～

As Pablo Picasso's fame grew, so did the attempts by other artists to forge Picasso paintings for profit. Picasso himself was often called upon to declare a painting an original or a fraud.

One painting that he called a fraud was proven to be painted by the master himself, as testified to by witnesses who had seen him paint it.

Picasso dismissed the matter in true genius style, declaring, "I can paint false Picassos as well as anyone."

During a public meeting, Nikita Khrushchev, premier of the Soviet Union, denounced Joseph Stalin for his murderous excesses. A voice from the audience demanded to know why Khrushchev didn't stop Stalin before his reign of terror destroyed so many people.

Khrushchev erupted in anger, shouting from the stage, "Who said that?"

No one said a word.

"Now you know why," Khrushchev explained.

~~~

When movie star Gary Cooper was ridiculed, at fifty-six, for playing the romantic interest of Audrey Hepburn, who was eighteen, in *Love in the Afternoon,* he went out and had a face lift.

~~~

Movie star Arnold Schwarzenegger recalled his bodybuilding days: "I was always interested in proportion and perfection. When I was fifteen, I took off my clothes and looked in the mirror. When I stared at myself naked, I realized that to be perfectly proportioned I would need twenty-inch arms to match the rest of me."

~~~

George C. Scott was infamous for his intense, intimidating personality. When an actress complained to director Mike Nichols that she was afraid of Scott, Nichols replied: "My dear, *everyone* is scared of George."

Wesley Snipes knocked director John Singleton for not casting him in the title role of the remake of *Shaft*, claiming the film would have doubled its box office if he had been the star.

⌇

Talleyrand, the eighteenth-century French statesman, once explained to another politician how to impress the French people: "You might try getting crucified and rising again on the third day."

⌇

When William F. Buckley sent Norman Mailer a copy of his newest book, Mailer turned to the index to see if Buckley had written about him.

Mailer found that Buckley had anticipated his response and handwritten the word "Hi!" next to Mailer's name in the index.

⌇

Madonna: "If I weren't as talented as I am ambitious, I would be a gross monstrosity."

⌇

General Douglas MacArthur spoke of himself in the third person and installed a fifteen-foot mirror behind his desk so he would look bigger to visitors.

MacArthur, who took the Pacific back from the Japanese during World War II, ordered photographers to shoot him from a low angle so he would appear taller in all photos.

Basketball star Dennis Rodman: "No one's going to tell me it's not manly to drive a pink truck or wear pink nails. I'll be the judge of my own manliness."

~~~~

At Woodstock, history's most famous rock concert, political radical Abbie Hoffman jumped up onstage and attempted to grab a mike and talk to the crowd.

Hoffman's mistake: He did it during a set by the Who. Singer Peter Townshend didn't believe in giving up the mike to anyone. He hit Hoffman on the head with his guitar, knocking him off the stage.

~~~~

"Oh, God, don't envy me," millionaire singer Barbra Streisand said. "I have my own pains."

~~~~

Where does the famous ego end?

Consider the opinion of biologist J. B. S. Haldane, observing the relationship of the uniquely human to the 400,000 species of beetles: "The Creator, if He exists, has a special preference for beetles."

CHAPTER 25

In the bath with the Beatles

The excesses of fame

If we want to keep the paparazzi in the dark, you and I have to dig our own tunnels. Tom Cruise doesn't.

That's because they do little things for the famous that no one will ever do for us.

~~~

When the Fab Four were bigger than Jesus, bigger even than Britney, an American company tried to buy the Beatles' bathwater so they could bottle it and sell it to fans.

The Beatles turned down the opportunity to cash in on a vast supply of used bathwater. But not everyone has said no when opportunity splashed.

The celebrity bathwater business began with Rudolph Valentino, the original matinee idol. Valentino's valet supplemented his salary by selling the star's bathwater to women fans at $20 a vial.

~~~

When Confucius died, his disciples built homes in the graveyard where he was buried and lived there for six years, mourning his death.

When Meryl Streep filmed *The French Lieutenant's Woman* on location in the English town of Lyme Regis, the townsfolk objected to the producer's request that they remove the TV antennas from their roofs so the town skyline would look Victorian again for the film.

The producer finally got his way by renting portable TV sets for everyone in town until the production was complete.

~~~~~

Actor Jack Webb, who played a police detective on TV's *Dragnet,* had his wedding cake covered in iced police badges.

~~~~~

Lucullus, wealthiest Roman of them all, held such elaborate feasts (and so often) that he kept files of party menus arranged by price so he could serve his guests according to their rank.

He also dressed for the ball from a wardrobe of five thousand purple robes, which meant he could go fourteen years without having to wear the same robe twice.

Wait, there's more Luculluses:

He once threw a chef in prison for an inferior sauce.

He kept tickle slaves, whose job it was to tickle his guests' throats with feathers so they would vomit up one huge meal in order to then consume another.

When Tiny Tim and Miss Vicki got married on the Johnny Carson show, the TV producers scattered about the stage a few tulips for the couple because the alternatively talented Tiny T. had become famous for singing (badly and accompanied more or less on the ukulele) the song, "Tiptoe Through the Tulips."

How many tulips? In true TV style of overdoing a non-event to make Lucullus proud of them: ten thousand tulips.

～～～

When Walter Matthau went to Florida to make a TV series, he lost $183,000 betting on spring-training baseball games.

By middle age Matthau estimated his lifetime gambling losses at $5 million.

～～～

Erich von Stroheim was known in Hollywood as a tough director. When filming *The Wedding March,* he worked actors and crew thirty to forty hours straight. He kept a hospital unit on the set, where the cast could recuperate between takes.

～～～

The artist Jasper Johns destroyed all his paintings and other creations at the age of twenty-four.

Then he started all over again and four years later had his first show.

WHAT THEY DO FOR THE FAMOUS THAT THEY DON'T DO FOR THE REST OF US

1. During the making of the movie *Interview with the Vampire*, the producers built a tunnel from the set to Tom Cruise's trailer so that he couldn't be photographed.

The studio wanted no vampire pictures of Cruise to be published until the movie opened.

2. A Bob Knight trading card edition was put out by Fleer that included a tiny piece of one of the hyper basketball coach's sweaters.

3. When movie star John Barrymore was too drunk to dance with costar Camilla Horn in a romantic ballroom scene during production of *The Tempest,* producers built a carousel for the couple.

"He sat on one side, me on the other," Camilla recalled. "We put our arms around each other, looked deeply into our eyes and somebody moved the carousel around so it looked in the film as if we were swirling around the ballroom lost in each other's arms."

4. Gilda Radner's writing partner Alan Zweibel helped her create her famous *Saturday Night Live* character Roseanne Roseannadanna.

They were both so caught up in the zany Roseannadanna that when they went anywhere together, "We'd both be Roseanne," Radner said.

When Radner was on camera performing a Roseannadanna skit, Zweibel would stand next to the camera.

"If he sees me slipping, he'll start to move his hands back and forth in Roseanne's rhythms," Radner said. "I look into the camera, but I'll see his stupid head bobbing back and forth on the side."

CHAPTER 26

The cowboy who went out west to Philadelphia

*People who are famous for
things they probably shouldn't be*

Movie stars who lip-synch while others sing. Scientists who take the credit for their students' research. All too common.

But when it comes to the limits of false fame, we have to look toward the man known as "Shut the Gates of Mercy."

The Heisman Trophy, college football's top honor, is given to the nation's player who best represents the prowess and ideals of the amateur game.

Ironically, the trophy was named for Georgia Tech coach John "Shut the Gates of Mercy" Heisman, who once allowed his team to run up 220 points against an outmanned opponent.

John Batterson Stetson, the man who invented the cowboy hat, was an easterner. He manufactured the hat on the west side of Philadelphia.

Cleopatra, Egypt's most famous queen, wasn't even Egyptian. Cleopatra was Greek, born into the family of one of Alexander the Great's generals. She was the first member of the royal family of Egypt to learn the Egyptian language.

In the movie about the life of Tina Turner, *What's Love Got to Do With It?*, Laurence Fishburne is convincing as the band's lead guitarist, Ike Turner. But he took the Hollywood practice of lip-synching to a new level: Fishburne was guitar-synching.

"I had a coach who made sure my fingers were in the right places on the guitar," he explained. "During the performing scenes, they played a tape of the song so we could stay on track."

Author James Fenimore Cooper became America's first hit novelist in the 1800s with *The Last of the Mohicans*, *The Deerslayer*, and other tales of frontier life in the wilderness.

Cooper's secret: He never went anywhere near the frontier, living his life in staid, conservative New York. He also defended slavery and opposed giving the vote to anyone but men who owned a lot of land.

Sergeant Alvin York, whose fighting prowess made him the great American hero of World War I, had tried to avoid the war by filing for conscientious objector status.

Singing cowboy star Gene Autry: "I'm not a good actor, a good rider, or a particularly good singer, but they seem to like what I do, so I'll keep on doing it as long as they want."

~~~

Colonel Sanders, one of Kentucky's most successful sons, produced one of the state's most famous products, Kentucky Fried Chicken. Only problem: He wasn't a colonel and wasn't from Kentucky.

~~~

Before the French writer Colette became famous in her own right, her husband, Henry Gauthier-Villars, signed his name to the first six books his wife wrote.

~~~

When Ray Ellis played in the Paul Whiteman Orchestra on TV, he claimed that conductor Paul Whiteman was just faking it for the camera, that the musicians actually followed a real conductor standing just off camera.

~~~

"Dixie," the song that lifted up the spirits of the Confederate troops during the Civil War, was written by a northerner, Dan Emmett.

~~~

Alan Ladd was a famous movie star, earning plenty of credits on his own. But he was incorrectly listed in the cast credits for the 1937 western *Born to the West*.

Ladd was never actually in the film, but it still shows up in his filmography, and he was listed in the credits on the video box.

Franz Mesmer was an Austrian physician who inadvertently developed hypnotism as a tool of healing.

Mesmer wasn't trying to hypnotize anyone. He thought his powers were supernatural, channeled through a little magnet which he kept hanging around his neck. To heal disease, Mesmer would magnetize everything from people to trees to bowls and plates.

~~~~

During the French Revolution, Dr. Joseph Guillotin received a grim notoriety for inventing the beheading device that bears his name. Only problem: Guillotin didn't invent the guillotine—another, never-famous doctor did.

Guillotin received all the credit because he campaigned for *use* of the guillotine throughout France.

Morbid? Perhaps, but Guillotin's motives were revolutionary: He wanted to create a society of equals, where all condemned could have their heads cut off. At that time, only nobility were beheaded. People of a lower class were hanged.

CHAPTER 27

So famous it hurts

The bitter taste of sweet fame

Vincent van Gogh sold a single painting in his entire life and died in poverty, his greatness unrecognized. His paintings have since made millions of dollars—for collectors and art dealers.

Such is the bittersweet possibilities of fame. If you think it only happened to van Gogh, read on.

Think you've had it rough when your hard drive crashes?

English historian Thomas Carlyle struggled for a year to write the first volume of his *History of the French Revolution*. He did it back in the old days when they wrote with pen and ink. No copy machines, not even carbon copies.

Finally finished, Carlyle gave his only manuscript to his friend and mentor, John Stuart Mill, for commentary.

Mill's maid thought it was waste paper and used the manuscript to start the kitchen fire.

No backups in the nineteenth century, so Carlyle had to write the manuscript all over again by hand, commenting that he felt like a man who has "nearly killed himself accomplishing zero."

J. S. Bach was not a famous composer in his own lifetime. After his death, some of his manuscripts were used as scrap paper. It took another fifty years before his genius was recognized.

Haven't you often felt that way?

~~~

When Herman Melville moved his family to a farm in 1850, the author thought he would make a good living as a farmer and writer. He failed at both.

His whaling saga, *Moby-Dick,* was rejected by critics and readers, and his farm went bankrupt.

Melville gave up, moved to New York and became a customs official, dying in obscurity. Not till thirty years after his death was *Moby-Dick* recognized as an American masterpiece.

~~~

Stephen Foster, one of America's greatest songwriters ("Oh, Susanna," "Camptown Races," and the sublime "Hard Times Come Again No More") died at the age of thirty-seven, with exactly 38 cents in his pocket.

~~~

Singer Ed Ames from the popular Ames Brothers returned from one of too many road trips. His young daughter met him at the door and called out, "Mommy, he's home."

"Who's home?" his wife asked.

His daughter answered, "One of the Ames Brothers."

PREJUDICE AND FAME

1. When black performers Louis Armstrong, Nat "King" Cole, and Sammy Davis Jr. starred in casino acts in Las Vegas in the 1940s and '50s, they were only stars onstage.

After their shows were done, they were ushered out the back doors (because black people weren't allowed through the front doors of Vegas casinos).

2. When singer Dorothy Dandridge, who was black, dipped her foot in a hotel pool in Vegas in the 1950s, the hotel management emptied the pool and refilled it so white guests could swim again.

3. In 1929, President Herbert Hoover's wife, Lou, invited the wife of a black congressman from Chicago to the White House. The Texas legislature immediately tried to impeach the president.

4. When Stan Getz, a white saxophone player, sat in with black bands in the segregated '50s, many of the clubs strung a rope down the middle of the room, keeping the white audience on one side and the black audience on the other.

5. When Lionel Hampton's band toured the South in the segregated '50s, its members hired a white bus driver, who could go into road stop restaurants and buy them a meal.

6. The Pointer Sisters went to Nashville to record country songs and were invited to a party at a southern mansion. When they arrived at the mansion, security guards assumed they were maids and sent them around to the back door.

Poet T. S. Eliot: "No one who ever won the Nobel Prize ever wrote anything worth reading afterwards."

~~~

By the time she was fifteen, singer Charlotte Church had recorded three albums of classical music and sold close to eight million copies.

By that time she was already fully aware of the downside of her success: "Not being home enough, being tired, having to be happy all the time. I'm on show 24-7, and I can never be in a bad mood, which is quite hard for a pretty moody teenager.

"And when the press writes 'the Maria Callas of Cardiff,' I'm like, that's a slightly dramatic comparison, since she was a great opera singer and I'm this little girl from Wales."

~~~

Bandleader Artie Shaw: "How many times can you play 'Begin the Beguine' without getting a little vomity?"

~~~

Actor Anthony Hopkins: "I've worked with geniuses and artists, and they're a nightmare. They're dull and deadly and suck all the life out of a film.

"You'd think they were talking about something really important. It's not, it's acting. It's all about entertainment. I can't associate myself with all the clatter that goes on around it."

~~~

They say New Orleans musician Buddy Bolden invented jazz in 1900. His band played jazz for seven years, after which Bolden was admitted to an asylum for the insane.

The great poems and stories of Edgar Allan Poe brought him neither reward nor comfort. Even though his most famous poem, "The Raven," was recognized as a work of genius while he was still alive, it took Poe a year to collect the payment from the New York paper that published it: $10.

Gilbert and Sullivan achieved fame and fortune with their numerous light operas, such as *The Mikado.* Why then so bitter?

Both of them considered these operas to be mere commercial works. They did it for the money. Nothing more. They held themselves as serious composers of far more important work—none of which was successful or is remembered today.

Scientist Charles Babbage died unrecognized for his life's work: designing a mechanical computer in the mid-1800s. Not till thirty years after his death was the computer pioneer recognized for his genius.

Franz Kafka died at forty. The two books that would make him famous *(The Trial* and *The Castle)* had not even been published at his death.

Singer Frankie Laine enjoyed great popularity, but late in his career, too late. "I scuffled for seventeen years before it happened," he said, "and seventeen is a bit much."

Philosopher Friedrich Nietzsche *(Thus Spake Zarathustra),* whose ideas went on to wield global influence, lived and died in poverty, wracked by disease, migraines, and insomnia and addicted to drugs. He spent the last eleven years of his life in an asylum. After his death, he became a cult figure.

Italian artist Amedeo Modigliani had only one exhibit of his paintings during his lifetime. It was shut down by the police, who called his female nudes obscene.

Anne Morrow did not seek fame. It came along with the heroic exploits of her husband, aviation pioneer Charles Lindbergh, and later the horror of the kidnapping of her young son, later still when she wrote her books.

All too quickly, she learned that while fame might give you access and ease, that would not add up to freedom.

"I was quite unprepared for this cops and robbers pursuit, an aspect of publicity that has become a common practice with public figures," she explained. "I felt like an escaped convict. This was not freedom."

French painter Paul Gauguin gave up the respectable life of a Parisian stockbroker to live the romantic life of an artist in Tahiti. There he painted some of the greatest works of all time—but not of his time. Gauguin's work was rejected by the art world, and he died in poverty.

Despite his genius, Wolfgang Mozart lived in poverty while lesser composers received the adulation, royal recognition, and wealth that accrue to those who have not great talent but great contacts.

Perhaps it is the critics who have gotten it all wrong—and man's greatest art is not music or poetry or paint but the talent for saying the right thing to the right people.

CHAPTER 28

So close and yet so ... who?

*People who had every right
to become famous but didn't*

What if Lana Turner had gone to the wrong soda fountain?
What if Alexander Graham Bell had taken the day off?

Then they would have joined the ranks of the almost
famous.

~~~~~

Pete Best, known as the Fifth Beatle, was bounced from the
band just before they became the hottest thing in rock 'n' roll.

After the Beatles became an international sensation, Pete
went on a gimmick tour with his own backup band, billing
himself as "Best of the Beatles."

Two decades later, Best couldn't stop pondering his fate
(could you?): "I still feel shocked," he said. "I'll never know why
it had to happen to me."

That sums up outrageous fortune: Whether it happens to
the famous, the infamous, or the forgotten, there's always
something unfair about it.

Everyone knows Alexander Graham Bell. He invented the telephone, which led to Ma Bell, pay phones, cell phones, and idiots in phone commercials.

But Ma Bell was almost Ma Gray.

Rival researcher Elisha Gray was independently inventing another telephone at the same time Bell did his work. Bell got to the patent office a few hours before Gray, and so it's all Bell and no Gray. Ouch.

～～～

Hockey coach Harry Neale might have become a coaching legend, if he could have solved his team's singular dilemma: "We couldn't win at home and we were losing on the road," he explained. "My failure as a coach was that I couldn't think of any place else to play."

～～～

Ron Necciai pitched the greatest game in baseball history: throwing a no-hitter in which all twenty-seven outs were strikeouts.

Why isn't he famous? He did it for a Class D Bristol team in the Appalachian League in 1952.

If he had pitched that incredible game in the majors, Necciai would have become a sports immortal instead of a trivia question.

Necciai did make it to the majors that same year, playing for the Pittsburgh Pirates. But at that level, which has tormented the almost-great for one hundred years, he was a bust.

Fame appreciates talent. But fame adores timing and luck.

At the same time Charles Darwin was making his discoveries about evolution, which would revolutionize our ideas about mankind's heritage, another scientist, Alfred Russel Wallace, was conducting the same experiments and coming to the same conclusions.

Even though Darwin wasn't racing Wallace and it took Darwin many years before he published the results of his studies, no one remembers Wallace today, and no one would object if you taught Wallacism in school.

~~~~

Rock 'n' roll has its one-hit wonders. Major league baseball has its one-game players, the cup-of-coffee guys who make the record books but with no impact, and only because baseball keeps such obsessive record books.

Henry Heitman was one of the oddest one-timers in baseball history. A pitcher, Heitman started one game for the Brooklyn Dodgers against St. Louis in 1918. He faced four batters, gave up four hits, was pulled out of the game, hit the showers, packed his grip, left the stadium, enlisted in the navy, and never played ball again.

~~~~

We all remember Casey Jones, the heroic engineer who died behind the throttle in a train crash. But who remembers the name of the railroad man who wrote that famous ballad? No one, probably because he sold the rights to the song for a bottle of gin.

Some athletes would be millionaire sensations because of their extraordinary skill—if only their skill played into a high-paying popular sport instead of the games of the obscure.

Take Ashrita Furman, who would have wowed the crowd packed around Manhattan's Central Park reservoir (if only there had been a crowd) in 1980 or won the Olympic gold for endurance gymnastics (if only there was such a competition) when he circled the entire ten-mile path doing somersaults.

Or how about Ted Allen, who had one of the most accurate arms in all of sports? Unfortunately, Allen applied his talents in one of the most obscure sports: horseshoes. Allen, a national champ throughout the 1930s and '40s, once threw 180 ringers in 200 throws.

On January 26, 1960, Danny Heater scored 135 points in a high school basketball game. In the NBA, entire teams most often don't score that much. But Heater never became an NBA star.

John Duns Scotus was a brilliant philosopher from Scotland in the thirteenth century. His ideas are now forgotten, but not the slurs of his detractors, for it's from Scotus, unfittingly, that we have derived the word *dunce*.

Sometimes you do everything right to become a legend, and it gets taken from you by the quirks of history.

Everyone assumes that the town of Pancake, Pennsylvania, was named for our favorite flapjacks. But it wasn't. The town was named for an early settler, George Pancake, who should have been famous but got beaten out by a breakfast food.

In the same way, the town of Conifer, Colorado, was not named for the tree but for a tavern keeper of the area, George Conifer.

～～～

Baseball should open a Hall of the Almost Famous for the stars who flash out of nowhere, then flash off just as quickly.

Take the sensational debut late in the 1940 season of Detroit rookie pitcher Floyd Giebell, who was sent to the mound in a critical game that would determine which team won the pennant.

Giebell went up against one of the greats, Cleveland's Bob Feller. The rookie out-pitched the veteran, 2-0, to win the pennant for the Tigers. But Giebell couldn't top that feat or sustain star status. He went on to win only two more games in his entire career.

Or how about Dodger first baseman Dick Nen, who hit the home run that clinched the 1963 pennant for L.A.?

Remember the name Dick Nen? Probably not, because his star drama lasted for the flight of that one long ball. That was the only homer he ever hit for the Dodgers.

CHAPTER 29

Do I want to star in one of the most popular movies of all time and win an Oscar? No thanks.

Stars who turned down roles you'd think only a fool would turn down

Casablanca without Bogie? Impossible. Bogie is Rick.

Yet if Hollywood had its way, Rick would have been, gasp, Ronald Reagan.

Does that mean Bogie would have ended up as president of the United States?

So many classic movies and great TV shows are linked with the stars who made those roles their own. Yet they were rarely the original choice. Consider these stars who turned down roles that made other actors famous:

Before Anne Bancroft seduced Dustin Hoffman in *The Graduate*, the role of the most famous older woman in film history was offered to Doris Day, who refused because the idea offended her.

Hard to believe anyone but Jack Nicholson could have played the lead role of McMurphy in *One Flew Over the Cuckoo's Nest*. But the star turn had been offered first to Marlon Brando, then Gene Hackman, then Burt Reynolds.

~~~

Gene Hackman was the first choice to play Mike Brady on *The Brady Bunch*.

Wouldn't you love to see just one episode of *The Brady Bunch* starring Gene Hackman? The nostalgic mind reels.

~~~

Holly Hunter turned down the lead that did so much for Helen Hunt's career in *As Good as It Gets*.

Then again, Debra Winger nixed the role that did so much for Holly Hunter's career in *Broadcast News*.

~~~

Actresses who refused to play Bonnie in *Bonnie and Clyde*, a role that made Faye Dunaway famous: Sue Lyon, Tuesday Weld, Jane Fonda.

~~~

Bridget Fonda was offered the title role on *Ally McBeal* but turned it down so she could make more movies. Fonda even refused to read the script, worried that she would like it too much to say no.

~~~

Marie Osmond turned down the lead role in the movie *Grease* on moral grounds.

Elvis Presley was going to play the Kris Kristofferson role in *A Star Is Born* with Barbra Streisand, but Elvis's manager, Colonel Tom Parker, refused to let the King act in a movie where his name wasn't top-listed in the credits.

~~~

The Godfather would have been a completely different film if either Robert Redford or Dustin Hoffman had said yes to the Al Pacino role of Michael Corleone.

How flexible is Hollywood (or how unsure of itself) when a role could be played by Al Pacino, Dustin Hoffman, or Robert Redford?

~~~

Al Pacino said no to *Pretty Woman* and *Crimson Tide*. Amazingly, he was also asked to play Han Solo in *Star Wars*.

Al Pacino in outer space? What were they thinking?

~~~

Shirley Temple was supposed to play Dorothy in *The Wizard of Oz*. But Shirley's studio, 20th Century Fox, refused to lend her to MGM, a common practice at a time when stars were under contract to a particular studio for life and could make only the movies assigned to them.

That's how Judy Garland got the part for which she is most remembered.

~~~

Chevy Chase was offered the Kevin Spacey lead in *American Beauty*. Didn't want it. Also saying no: Tom Hanks.

Clint Eastwood was the ultimate Dirty Harry, the cop who made his own rules, in a series of tough crime movies, but he wasn't the first choice.

John Wayne, Frank Sinatra, and Paul Newman all turned down the Dirty Harry role, with Newman suggesting Eastwood for the role that defined his career.

~~~~

Cher could have played Thelma in *Thelma & Louise*. Well, she could have had the role. Whether she could have played it, we'll never know.

~~~~

Ben Kingsley won an Oscar as Best Actor for *Gandhi*. Who turned down the chance? Alec Guinness, Anthony Hopkins, Albert Finney, Peter Finch, and Dirk Bogarde.

~~~~

Peter Finch won an Oscar for playing the crazy newscaster in *Network*. But he wouldn't have won anything if any of three other actors had said yes when offered the part before Finch: Henry Fonda, Glenn Ford, George C. Scott.

~~~~

The original cast of *The Bridge on the River Kwai* almost included Humphrey Bogart, Laurence Olivier, and Cary Grant. Just as well it didn't.

~~~~

Robert De Niro declined the role of Jesus in *The Last Temptation of Christ*. A De Niro Christ probably would not have turned the other cheek.

Kirk Douglas turned down two roles that won Best Actor Oscars for other actors: Lee Marvin in *Cat Ballou* and William Holden in *Stalag 17*. Kirk never did win his own Oscar for Best Actor.

Jodie Foster turned down the Sharon Stone role in *Basic Instinct*. Foster got the role of Clarice Starling in *The Silence of the Lambs* only after Michelle Pfeiffer turned it down.

Chris O'Donnell, who played Robin in two Batman movies, turned down the role in *Men in Black* that made a star of Will Smith.

Hedy Lamarr turned down the Ingrid Bergman part in *Casablanca*.

Robert Redford said no to the part that made Dustin Hoffman famous in *The Graduate*.

W. C. Fields refused to play the wizard in *The Wizard of Oz*.

CHAPTER 30

"Louie Louie" a rock 'n' roll song? Or an attempt to subvert the government of the USA?

When they got it wrong about famous people

You never know who is going to become famous next, maybe even that jerk at work.

So before you predict failure and obscurity for that idiot, remember the words of the absurdist playwright Eugene Ionesco: "You can only predict things after they have happened."

~~~~

When he was filming *The Sound of Music*, star Christopher Plummer thought the musical was going to be awful, so he scornfully called it *The Sound of Mucus*.

In 1961, the FBI investigated the rock 'n' roll group the Kingsmen for acts of national subversion in their song with the puzzling lyrics: "Louie Louie."

Poet T. S. Eliot, while working for a publishing house, rejected George Orwell's *Animal Farm*. So did twenty-two other book publishers.

When finally published, *Animal Farm* became a classic satire still taught widely in schools.

Animal Farm was not the only best-selling book that almost had no sales at all because publishers rejected it.

Take the story of one Theodor Geisel, who had his first book rejected by twenty-three publishers before it was finally accepted and went on to sell millions of copies, as did all of his other books.

Sound familiar? Geisel was Dr. Seuss, and that first book was *And to Think That I Saw It on Mulberry Street*.

Other best-selling books initially turned down by people in the publishing business who should have known better: *Dune* (thirteen rejections), *Auntie Mame* (seventeen), *M*A*S*H* (twenty-one), James Joyce's *The Dubliners* (twenty-two), *The Peter Principle* (sixteen), *Kon-Tiki* (twenty).

EVEN THE FAMOUS DON'T GET IT WHEN IT'S THEIR OWN WORK

1. "I feel strongly that what you want me to do is not an important picture. You promised me that you would not require me to perform in anything but important pictures."

That's George Raft turning down the Humphrey Bogart role in the immortal mystery *The Maltese Falcon*.

2. "I know what's funny, and this isn't funny." Barbra Streisand on *What's Up, Doc?* one of her funniest movies, or audiences thought so.

3. "There is no difference between doing this kind of film and playing King Lear. The actor's job is exactly the same: Dress up and pretend."

That's Harrison Ford's opinion on *Return of the Jedi*, the first, and probably the only, time *Star Wars* was compared with Shakespearean tragedy.

Then there are the professional critics who get paid to get it wrong.

Newspapers don't send critics out to cover the day's work at the local moving company, so the only people who know how badly Joe lugs around the china are the people whose china he has dropped.

But if Joe was a movie star playing a china-dropping mover, we'd have pros around the country analyzing his every move.

Meanwhile, the critics got it wrong about these stars and their movies:

1. Here's a young actor tossed on the scrap heap of bit players as just another "standard issue baby-faced actor" by critic David Danby of *New York* magazine in 1983.

Which long-forgotten bad actor is Danby talking about? Tom Cruise.

2. This interesting critic said more about herself than the movie—Dorothy Thompson of the *New York Herald Tribune* wrote in 1940: "I left the theater in a condition bordering on nervous breakdown (from) this remarkable nightmare."

What horror film was she talking about? Walt Disney's beloved cartoon *Fantasia*.

3. "With *Annie Hall,* Woody Allen has truly under-reached himself. It is a film so shapeless, sprawling, repetitious, and aimless as to seem to beg for oblivion," wrote John Simon in *New York* magazine.

Who knows what movie Simon saw? *Annie Hall* is Woody's most oblivion-resistant masterpiece. So say fans and the Academy of Motion Pictures, which gave *Annie Hall* the Oscar for Best Picture.

4. Plenty of critics pounced on Woody Allen early in his career, going out of their way to make themselves look foolish.

Here's *Commentary* magazine critic William Pechter giving himself twenty-seven years to get it wrong about Woody in a 1973 review of *Sleeper:* "Given that rate of progress toward comic charisma, Woody Allen might just inch his way past the Three Stooges by the year 2000."

I love the Three Stooges, but Woody must be the world's fastest incher.

5. Critic John Simon seemed to confuse writing about movies with a visit to his analyst, as he went after stars the way Oedipus went after the king:

About Diane Keaton (in *Annie Hall*): "Not so much an actress playing a role as a soul in torment crying out for urgent therapy, in bad taste to watch and an indecency to display."

About Liza Minnelli (in *Cabaret*): "Plain, ludicrously rather than pathetically plain is what Miss Minnelli is."

About Barbra Streisand (in *What's Up, Doc?*): "Miss Streisand looks like a cross between an aardvark and an albino rat surmounted by a platinum-coated horse bun."

About Streisand again (in *Up the Sandbox*): "I cannot accept a romantic heroine who is both knock-kneed and ankleless . . . short-waisted and shapeless, scrag-toothed and with a horse face centering on a nose that looks like Brancusi's Rooster cast in liverwurst."

Streisand-bashing again (in *The Way We Were*): "She cannot conquer our impression that, were she to collide with a Mack truck, it is the truck that would drop dead."

Yet again (in *Funny Lady*): "There may be uglier women in the world than she is, but surely none that wears her ugliness, enhanced by monumental arrogance, with more bravura."

Oh, how Streisand's continued success must have galled Simon.

CHAPTER 31

From Thomas Edison's breath to Bogie's whistle

The final exits of famous people

"I don't want to achieve immortality through my work," Woody Allen said. "I want to achieve it through not dying."

We can't help Woody with that one, but we can track some famous exits.

~~~

Auto magnate Henry Ford was bedside with his friend Thomas Edison when the inventor died in 1931. Ford brought a bottle with him, into which Edison exhaled as he expired.

Ford then kept his friend's dying breath until his own death sixteen years later.

~~~

Roy Rogers: "When I die, just skin me out and put me up on old Trigger and I'll be happy." (That may be the cowboy's dream way to go, but, no, it didn't happen.)

~~~

Death is easy, as Russian revolutionary Leon Trotsky knew: "Old age is the most unexpected of all things that happen to a man."

When husband Humphrey Bogart died, actress Lauren Bacall put something in Bogie's coffin: a small, gold whistle. If you have to ask why, you haven't seen enough great old movies.

~~~

As Italian artist Amedeo Modigliani lay dying in Paris, he asked his teenage lover, model and art student Jeanne Hebuterne, to die with him so he could have "my favorite model in paradise and with her enjoy eternal happiness."

On the day of his funeral, pregnant with Modigliani's child, Jeanne jumped to her death.

~~~

Upon his death bed, comic actor W. C. Fields lay reading a Bible, which surprised his friends, since the curmudgeonly Fields was a confirmed agnostic. Fields explained: "I'm looking for a loophole."

~~~

Some people hold onto a treasured keepsake from a loved one who has passed on. Same for the famous, although their keepsakes may tend toward the bizarre:

After Sir Walter Raleigh was executed and beheaded, his body was buried—but his widow held onto his head for twenty-nine years, keeping it in a velvet bag.

~~~

America's great humorist Will Rogers saw the progress of death this way: "You can't say civilization don't advance, for in every war they kill you in a new way."

EARLY DEATHS OF FAMOUS PEOPLE

As the poet Byron (who died at thirty-six) said, "Those whom the gods love, die young."

1. Rock idols who died before they turned thirty: Jimi Hendrix, Jim Morrison, Janis Joplin, Otis Redding, Buddy Holly, Sam Cooke, Duane Allman, Brian Jones (Rolling Stones), Brian Cole (the Association), Ron Pigpen McKernan (the Grateful Dead), Marc Bolan (T. Rex).

2. Movie idols who died before they turned thirty-seven: James Dean, Jayne Mansfield, Marilyn Monroe, Jean Harlow, Rudolph Valentino.

3. Artists who died before they turned forty: Toulouse-Lautrec, Raphael, Modigliani, Caravaggio, Aubrey Beardsley, Seurat, and van Gogh. Jackson Pollock died at forty-four.

4. Writers who died before they turned forty: Dylan Thomas, Thomas Wolfe, Arthur Rimbaud, Robert Burns, Hart Crane, Stephen Crane, Sylvia Plath, Christopher Marlowe, Alfred Jarry, J. M. Synge, Emily Brontë, John Keats, Percy Shelley, Lord Byron.

Jack London, Edgar Allan Poe, and Franz Kafka outlived them and died at forty.

Although she lived a long life, writer and notorious wit Dorothy Parker was fascinated with death. She subscribed to the trade magazine for funeral parlors. When she learned that undertakers used a tuberose scent on corpses, she ordered some and used it as perfume.

~

Ben Jonson, one of Shakespeare's rivals as a playwright, beseeched King Charles I for a square foot in Westminster Abbey. The king agreed, and Jonson was buried vertically to take up no more than a square foot of that space.

~

Writer Virginia Woolf, afraid she was going mad, killed herself by filling her pockets with stones and jumping into a river.

~

After dying in debt while failing to finish one his greatest compositions, "Requiem," Wolfgang Mozart had no attendants at his funeral, as a massive rainstorm kept wife and friends away. His body was dumped in a pauper's grave unmarked.

~

When actress Rachel Roberts committed suicide, director Otto Preminger said he wasn't surprised, then clarified his remark: "I wouldn't be surprised with half the actors I have known."

Rock 'n' roll singer Dion of Dion and the Belmonts was on tour with Buddy Holly and Ritchie Valens the night of their fatal plane crash. Buddy asked Dion to fly with them because the more people on their rented plane, the cheaper the fare for each of them.

Dion turned them down and, therefore, lived. "I was cheap," he explained. "I didn't want to spend anything extra."

~~~

When Japanese writer Yukio Mishima wrote his name, he used Japanese characters that also meant "mysterious devil entranced with death."

The militaristic Mishima committed ritual suicide at the height of his fame.

BEST FINAL WORDS

Much competition here, as famous people have a knack for famous last words, thinking always—even thinking last—of their biographers and their legends.

But my favorite for spirit and unflagging honesty goes to the great sixteenth-century French writer and scholar François Rabelais, who from his deathbed called out, "Ring down the curtain, the farce is over. I go to seek the great perhaps."

CHAPTER 32

Celebrity fleas and a better class of insult

Famous people talk about the nature of fame

Fame is a yo-yo. Or maybe it's a roller coaster. Up or down, come along for the ride.

Up: Sylvester Stallone: "Once in one's life, for one mortal moment, one must make a grab for immortality. If not, one has not lived."

Down: Actor Ronald Colman: "Fame has robbed me of my freedom and shut me up in prison, and because the prison walls are gilded and the key that locks me in is gold does not make it any more tolerable."

Up: Barbra Streisand: "Success to me is having ten honeydew melons and eating only the top half of each one."

Down: Greta Garbo: "Being a movie star, and this applies to all of them, means being looked at from every possible direction. You are never left at peace, you're just fair game."

Up: Actor Anthony Hopkins: "It beats working for a living."

Down: Cartoonist and playwright Jules Feiffer: "David Mamet is perhaps our foremost playwright. Which means that in today's world he is practically unknown."

ODD OBSERVATIONS ABOUT FAME

Lily Tomlin: "I've always wanted to be somebody, but I see now I should've been more specific."

When Walt Disney was asked about the advantages of celebrity, he observed: "It doesn't seem to keep fleas off our dogs. And if being a celebrity won't give one an advantage over a couple of fleas, then I guess there can't be much in being a celebrity."

Perhaps they were celebrity fleas.

Joan Rivers in 1980 on why there were few women stand-up comics: "It's a very lonely life on the road, and I think a lot of girls, after doing it for a little while, realize how horrendous it is. You stop because it's just too awful."

Jodie Foster's only regret: "I would love to live life without knowing what it's like to be famous."

Gene Hackman: "I was trained to be an actor, not a star. I was trained to play roles, not to deal with fame and agents and lawyers and the press."

Movie star Elsa Lanchester: "To complain too bitterly of the load of mischief that notoriety brings with it would mean that you are unsuited to the position you have made for yourself."

~~~

Roger Daltry of the Who about going on a major rock 'n' roll tour: "Your whole life is magnified, and yet you are trapped in this little insular group. Everything is out of proportion. You become more important than you are."

~~~

Grace Kelly: "Hollywood amuses me. Holier-than-thou for the public and unholier-than-the-devil in reality."

~~~

About his reputation as a brawler, basketball star Charles Barkley: "Fans believe what they see on TV or what they read. That's my problem with the media. Complete strangers come up to me and say: 'Don't punch me.'"

~~~

McDonald's king Ray Kroc about his fortune: "So what? I can still only wear one pair of shoes at a time."

~~~

Singer Sammy Davis Jr. back in the 1960s: "Being a star has made it possible for me to get insulted in places where the average Negro could never hope to go and get insulted."

~~~

Actor Sean Connery: "More than anything else, I'd like to be an old man with a good face, like Hitchcock or Picasso."

Writer/director Lawrence Kasdan *(The Big Chill)* said about the stars, "There's no connection between your value to the world and what you're paid. So there's this massive dissociation from any reality. I think it confuses people. You tend to become defensive or you begin to believe praise, which is just as dangerous."

Movie star Susan Sarandon: "I choose projects I can talk about for days because now you do publicity for as long as it took you to shoot the movie."

Author Carlos Fuentes puts it all in perspective: "You don't have too much time to stop and say, 'Hey, I'm a celebrity,' because such things mean nothing in the face of death."

CHAPTER 33

What does God have to say to Harrison Ford?

*Strange, ironic moments
in the lives of famous people*

When movie star Charlie Chaplin was traveling, he ran into a Chaplin look-alike competition. He entered. Came in third.

How ironic. But when it comes to celebrities, irony rules.

~~~~~

What do the sluggers Babe Ruth, Ted Williams, Stan Musial, and George Sisler have in common (other than being four of the best hitters ever to play the game)?

They all began in baseball as pitchers and were switched to other positions because of their prowess with the bat.

But if the designated hitter rule had been in effect when they played, we might never have known what great hitters they were.

Dooley Wilson is famous for one thing: playing the piano in Rick's cafe in the movie *Casablanca*. Ironically, Wilson could not play the piano and "As Time Goes By" was dubbed over, so he never got to play it again.

~~~

The Earl of Cardigan sent hundreds of brave British horsemen to their pointless deaths in what became more famous as a slaughter than it would have been as a victory, the Charge of the Light Brigade.

Despite the stupidity of that command to ride straight into the entrenched position of a superior enemy force, Cardigan became a national hero in England. Some kind of belated ironic justice was served, however, when he died years later from falling off a horse.

~~~

In the 1966 movie *Who's Afraid of Virginia Woolf?* Elizabeth Taylor and Richard Burton, married in real life, play an ever-battling couple whose marriage is a disaster.

Offscreen, their real marriage eroded and never recovered from the confrontational film, and they divorced in 1974.

Another victim of the film: costar Sandy Dennis, who played a supporting role while pregnant but lost the baby when filming ended. Did the film's hysterics play a part in that loss? Who can say?

When Christopher Columbus led his three ships across the Atlantic on his first voyage, his crews were nervous about how far they had traveled from known land. So Columbus kept two records of their journey: his personal estimates of how far they'd traveled, and a second journal he shared with the crew, which recorded the distances as far less.

Ironically, when later measured accurately, it turned out that the distances he made up were much closer to the truth.

~~~~

If you think TV gets boring now, you should have seen the world's first broadcast, when engineer Ernst Alexanderson demonstrated his invention in 1928.

How entertaining was that first TV show? A man took off his glasses and blew smoke rings.

Luckily for Alexanderson, he invented TV before newspapers invented TV critics.

~~~~

The Museum of Modern Art hung a Matisse painting upside down for forty-seven days before an art student noticed the mistake.

~~~~

Odds are that all-time home-run king Hank Aaron would have hit the first homer when the Braves moved to Atlanta Stadium. But he didn't. That honor went to his brother Tommie. Over their careers, Hank hit 755 home runs; Tommie thirteen.

Race car driver Dan Gurney won plenty of races with the fastest car on the track. But he also won one driving the slowest.

Happened this way: 1961, Daytona, last lap of the race. Gurney was way ahead in his Lotus, going to win easily when his engine died. Totally dead, with Gurney stranded only yards from the finish line.

As other cars raced to close in on him, Gurney desperately tried to start his engine. But nothing happened when he turned the ignition key. Well, not completely nothing. The car lurched forward a few feet.

Thinking quickly, Gurney flicked the key again, lurched forward two feet closer to the line. And he kept flicking and lurching across the finish line, traveling maybe one mile an hour, inching across to victory ahead of the cars traveling 180 times as fast.

When explorer Hernando Cortés suggested to King Charles V of Spain in the 1500s that they build a canal across the Isthmus of Panama, the king declined, saying, "What God hath joined together let no man put asunder."

The king hadn't figured on Americans, who make a national pastime out of putting asunder anything God dared join together.

The first Indy 500 was won by Ray Harroun, the only driver in the 1911 race who didn't have a mechanic sitting next to him.

Two years before Marlon Brando declined his Oscar for Best Actor in the 1972 movie *The Godfather,* he asked the Academy to replace the Oscar statue he won for *On the Waterfront* in 1954, which had been stolen.

~~~

David Geffen became one of the most powerful hit-makers in pop music and movies. But when he was struggling to break into the agenting business, he lied on his resume that he'd graduated from prestigious UCLA.

Years later, as a millionaire and one of the most powerful men in Hollywood, he was asked to join the Board of Regents at UCLA, a school he'd never attended.

~~~

Actress Margot Kidder, who starred as Lois Lane in the movie *Superman,* never read a Superman comic until the day before she auditioned for the part.

~~~

Harrison Ford (when asked, "If heaven exists, what would you want God to say to you at the pearly gates?"): "You're a lot better looking in person."

And what would you like God to say to *you* when you arrive?

I'd settle for: "Now the real adventure begins."

CHAPTER 34

Alexander won't drink

Nobility and grace among the famous

Nobility, sweetness, thoughtfulness—among the famous? Rare as they may be, we do find acts of celebrated grace.

~~~

William Gilbert, of Gilbert and Sullivan fame, died as a hero, trying to save a drowning girl when he was seventy-five years old.

~~~

After the Civil War, General Robert E. Lee refused to capitalize on his fame by writing his memoirs, declaring that if he did, "I should be trading on the blood of my men."

~~~

Leonidas, Spartan king in 480 B.C., led three hundred of his followers in a final stand against a huge Persian army, refusing all offers to surrender.

Over their common grave is written these inspirational words: "Stranger, go tell the Spartans that here, obedient to their command, we lie."

The town of Rugby was founded by Thomas Hughes, the Englishman who wrote *Tom Brown's School Days,* specifically to house the younger sons of wealthy Britons because these sons were forbidden by law from inheriting their father's property.

～～～

Union organizer Joe Hill was killed by a firing squad in Utah in 1915. Before he walked to his death, he sent a telegram to fellow union man Bill Haywood: "I will die like a true-blue rebel. Don't waste any time in mourning. Organize."

～～～

They say an army travels on its belly, but what about its generals?

Alexander the Great demonstrated his touch for brilliant leadership during an arduous trek across a desert. With his men struggling against thirst, Alexander was offered water by one of his soldiers.

Instead of drinking, Alexander asked the soldier if there was enough water for the entire army. When the soldier said there was not, Alexander poured the water into the sand.

～～～

Cardinal Francis Joseph Spellman shortened his nightly prayer when exhausted: "Dear God, you know I've been working in your vineyard all day. If you don't mind, could we skip the details till morning?"

One reason the Duke of Wellington defeated Napoleon at Waterloo was his ability to remain calm under pressure, even at the risk of his own life.

One day a madman who had escaped from an asylum broke into Wellington's office, announcing that he must kill the general.

Wellington looked up from his papers and inquired, "Does it have to be today?"

When the assassin hesitated, Wellington said, "A little later on, then. I'm busy at the moment."

The man left and was arrested, and Wellington got back to his work.

Over dinner, Alice Vanderbilt, wife of the millionaire Cornelius Vanderbilt, found out that her daughter-in-law had no pearls of her own because her son felt he couldn't afford good ones.

Alice immediately took the pearls from around her own neck, cut off a third of the strand and gave them to the young bride, informing her that "all Vanderbilt women have pearls."

Australia's great rower Henry Pearce was leading in the 1928 Olympic finals of the sculling event when a mother duck and her babies crossed the river in front of him. He pulled up oars and waited till they passed—and still won the gold.

WHAT DO THESE FAMOUS PEOPLE HAVE IN COMMON?

Scientist Isaac Newton; Clara Barton (founder of the Red Cross, known as "the angel of the battlefield"); singers Jimmy Buffett, Little Richard, Annie Lennox, Tony Martin, and Cab Calloway; baseball stars Nelli Fox and Rickey Henderson; football stars Larry Csonka, Kenny Stabler, and Kyle Rote Jr.; actors Sissy Spacek and Humphrey Bogart; artist Maurice Utrillo; hotel magnate Conrad Hilton; mystic Carlos Castaneda; and legendary rock producer Phil Spector.

They were all born on Christmas Day.

When the Greek philosopher Socrates was condemned to death for corrupting the youth of Athens, he had a unique answer to a supporter's complaint that the charge was unjust.

"Would you prefer it to be just?" Socrates countered.

Hannibal, the great general from Carthaginia, defeated the Romans in battle for fifteen years, despite being outnumbered all that time.

When he finally took poison rather than be captured as an old man, his enemies paid tribute to Hannibal's leadership: "He never required others to do what he could not and would not do himself."

~~~

General Douglas MacArthur showed his personal courage in odd ways during World War I: He would lead charges against the German trenches without helmet, gas mask, or gun, carrying only a riding crop.

It was not clear what MacArthur intended to do if he actually reached the German trenches, but you have to admire his guts.

CHAPTER 35

Hef, watch out for those astonished women

They said what?!

Paul Newman battles his salad dressing. William F. Buckley prepares to challenge victory. Robin Williams listens to God. Whenever famous people have something strange to say, we'll be there.

FAMOUS SELF-DOUBT

The more talented you are, the greater your insecurity: You know you're not responsible for creating the talent. It's something that happened to you. And you don't know when it will stop happening.

Movie star Katharine Hepburn: "I think most of the people involved in any art always secretly wonder whether they are really there because they're good—or because they're lucky."

Director Frank Capra *(It's a Wonderful Life):* "Behind every successful man there stands an astonished woman."

~~~~

Singer/actress Cher: "Some years I'm the coolest thing that ever happened, and the next year everyone's so over me."

~~~~

Isaac Newton, the scientific genius who discovered the law of gravity and motion, differential calculus, and theories of light and color, summed up his extensive accomplishments this way: "I do not know what I may appear to the world, but to myself I seem to have been only a boy playing on the sea-shore and diverting myself in now and then, finding a smoother pebble or a prettier shell than ordinary, whilst the great ocean of truth lay all undiscovered before me."

So how are you and I doing at the seashore?

~~~~

Actor/food company executive Paul Newman: "The embarrassing thing is that my salad dressing is outgrossing my films."

~~~~

Movie star Michelle Pfeiffer: "I still think people will find out that I'm really not very talented. I'm really not very good. It's all just been a big sham."

Pop singer Rod Stewart about his first touch of fame, as lead singer with the Faces: "I can't listen to those records. The Faces sound so out of tune, so out of time. We never had the musicianship. We did not come together as a band."

Actor/director Robert Redford: "As a director, I wouldn't like me as an actor. As an actor, I wouldn't like me as a director."

CELEBRITIES OBSESS ABOUT GROWING OLD

They fear they will lose to age what they have in the prime of their glory. So do the rest of us, only we never had that much to begin with.

When Jack Nicholson saw the teens-play-hooky comedy *Ferris Bueller's Day Off,* he lamented: "That movie made me feel totally irrelevant, 119 years old. I literally walked out of there thinking: My days are numbered in the Hollywood film industry."

Jane Fonda: "I was terrified when I turned thirty. I was pregnant and had the mumps and Faye Dunaway was just coming out in *Bonnie and Clyde.* I thought: Oh, my God, I'll never work again. I'm old!"

CELEBRITIES OBSESS
ABOUT THEIR FANS

Without fans, they have no fame. With fans, they have no privacy. Here's how some celebrities struggle with that love/hate relationship:

~~~

Saturday Night Live actress Gilda Radner on the packaging of fame: "One of the strangest things to me is when little children look at me and say, 'Gilda Radner!' like Scott Towels or Snickers candy. It's like a brand name to them."

~~~

Hollywood screenwriter Anita Loos: "So after a star has received five or six million of those fan letters, you begin to realize you must be wonderful without having to read all those monotonous letters."

~~~

Writer Arthur Koestler: "Liking a writer and then meeting the writer is like liking goose liver and then meeting the goose."

~~~

Child actress Shirley Temple: "I stopped believing in Santa Claus when my mother took me to see him in a department store and he asked for my autograph."

~~~

Actor Jack Nicholson: "The average celebrity meets, in one year, ten times the amount of people that the average person meets in his entire life."

Child actor Mickey Rooney: "The audience and I are friends. They allowed me to grow up with them. I've let them down several times. They've let me down several times. But we're all family."

~~~

Baseball slugger Mike Schmidt about how hard it is to hit when the fans are booing: "Baseball takes touch, timing, good eyesight, concentration. The fans should be forced to be quiet when you walk up to hit."

~~~

Rocker Bob Seger: "I really like the level of celebrity I have. I feel sorry for people like Michael Jackson and Bruce Springsteen. The first thing that happened when Bruce got huge, I said: Okay, ask him where he goes for a hamburger now."

~~~

Baseball star Jose Canseco evaluating the New York fans: "You could throw raw meat out there and they'll eat it. It's wild. *Wild Kingdom.*"

~~~

Phyllis Diller in 1980 about some of the more unusual ramifications of show-biz success: "There are probably a thousand homosexuals who regularly impersonate me at parties or in small clubs. And there are women who dress up and go to parties as me. If you produce a strong character, which I do, you are easy to imitate."

THE GOOD, THE BAD, AND THE WEIRD

Some surprising revelations about the odd trappings of fame:

~~~

Playboy publisher Hugh Hefner, denying he lived as a hermit while driving the magazine to the top: "I was a guy living a wild 24-hour-a-day life in a 45-room mansion with the whole best part of the world brought to him, including the wine, women, and song. Not too much singing, as I recall."

~~~

Basketball great Wilt Chamberlain: "I water ski at over 100 miles an hour. When I drive my cars, I've gone as much as 180 miles an hour. Most people dream of doing those things but never have enough nerve, maybe, to try them."

~~~

Writer Henry Miller: "A real artist doesn't want fame. All he wants is room enough to move around in and do what he likes. But all the rest—money, fame, success—all these are just as bad as nonrecognition and poverty and hunger."

~~~

Boxing champion Muhammad Ali on an airplane, not wanting to buckle his seat belt: "Superman don't need no seat belt."

The flight attendant: "Superman don't need no airplane." (Ali buckled up.)

Actor Robert Morley: "If you read a book about someone who had all these marvelous things happen to them, or they made a fortune, or they climbed Everest, or sailed around the world, and then they're dead when you're reading it, you'll feel a little bit better. But I can't die just to improve the sales of my book; that would be unfair."

〜

Comic actress and director Penny Marshall on how hard it was to make the hit TV comedy *Laverne and Shirley* (costarring Cindy Williams): "That's Cindy's complaint too: I can't date anymore. I'm exhausted. Where's my social life? You don't have one. This is it, you do this. Once in a while you go to one of those fancy parties you have to go to and say hello to all the other tired actors."

〜

English rocker Joe Jackson, one of the new wave's first hit-makers, turned his back on fame to become a classical composer: "The industry gives no credit to people who have long careers and more to say than a two-minute hit single. There's an insatiable appetite for new faces. The pop crowd is a monster that feeds on novelty."

GREAT COMEBACKS

Many celebrities had to fight their way to the top, so it's not surprising they're pretty good in a duel with the verbal thrusts and parries.

Walt Garrison played fullback for the champion Dallas Cowboys. When asked if legendary coach Tom Landry ever smiled, Garrison had to admit: "I don't know. I only played there nine years."

~

After *Psycho*'s shower scene scared Americans where they'd never been scared before—in their bathrooms—a man wrote to director Alfred Hitchcock to complain that his wife would no longer take a shower or bath.

Hitch wrote back: "Sir, have you considered sending your wife to the dry cleaners?"

~

Here's a political response that should be mandatory for most politicians. When conservative William F. Buckley ran for mayor of New York City to drum up new material for his newspaper column, he was asked what he'd do if he actually won. "Demand a recount," he replied quite reasonably.

~

When asked if she had anything on during a photo session, movie star Marilyn Monroe responded: "Sure, I had the radio on."

~

The great French writer Voltaire was once surrounded by an angry London mob, who threatened to hang him simply for being French. He turned the mob to his side with a simple judgment they could not deny: "You wish to kill me because I am a Frenchman? Am I not punished enough in not being born an Englishman?"

Playwright George Bernard Shaw once turned to a pompous dinner companion and said, "Between the two of us we know all there is to know."

The man assumed flattery, until Shaw explained, "You know everything except that you're a bore, and I know that."

SPORTS RETORTS

Sports, because there's so much bench time involved, is a place where great competitors work on their retorts the way they work on the swings. Consider these Hall of Fame cuts:

~~~

Indiana basketball coach Bobby Knight usually wasn't so kind, but here he is finding something positive to say about his enemies: "Absolute silence, that's the one thing a sportswriter can quote accurately."

~~~

Light-hitting catcher Joe Garagiola had a bad game one day, striking out, then hitting into a double play the next time up. As he returned to the dugout, lippy manager Leo Durocher suggested, "Why don't you strike out next time and keep the inning going."

Baseball great Pete Rose to his injured teammate Tony Perez: "How can anyone who runs as slow as you pull a muscle?"

~~~

Baseball star Graig Nettles on what it was like to play in New York: "When I was little, I wanted to be a baseball player and join the circus. With the Yankees, I've accomplished both."

FAMOUS PEOPLE SAY THE WEIRDEST THINGS, THANK YOU VERY MUCH

Odd things famous people uttered within hearing range of people who write such things down:

~~~

Bogie: "The trouble with the world is that it's always one drink behind."

~~~

Babe Herman was a baseball immortal and not just because of what he did on the field. Here he is talking about shopping for his son's birthday: "Buy an encyclopedia for my kid? He'll learn to ride a two-wheeler or walk."

~~~

Robert Mitchum: "Movies bore me, especially my own."

~~~

Comic Robin Williams: "Cocaine is God's way of telling you, you are making too much money."

Baseball pitcher David Cone on why he liked playing for the New York Mets: "I am borderline berserk. But I think New York understands borderline berserk. I think New York respects borderline berserk."

~~~~

Boxing champ Muhammad Ali: "Everybody says they'll marry till death, and they're divorced a few weeks later. I've lied to the judge twice myself."

~~~~

Actress Holly Hunter: "Acting, for me, is the last vestige of doing something that I would like to feel really naive about."

~~~~

Movie director Mel Brooks: "My movies rise below vulgarity."

~~~~

Kirk Douglas: "Virtue is not photogenic. What is it to be a nice guy? To be nothing, that's what. A big fat zero with a smile for everybody."

~~~~

Poet Edwin Arlington Robinson: "The world is not a prison house but a kind of kindergarten, where millions of bewildered infants are trying to spell God with the wrong blocks."

~~~~

Winston Churchill: "Nothing is so exhilarating as to be shot at without result."

~~~~

My favorite Elvis saying: "I don't know anything about music. In my line you don't have to."

PART 2

~~~~~~

INSIDE FAME

The questions you probably wanted to ask about fame if only you knew someone famous and, no, your cousin who was in the Weedwacker infomercial doesn't count

Please step out of our light. We're trying to be famous here.

Oh, you want to be famous too? You want the thrill, the glory, not to mention the paycheck?

But have you considered what you're going to do with your toy monkey?

Maybe you had better take a tour of the famous psyche before you step into the spotlight with us.

ARE THE FAMOUS JUST LIKE YOU AND ME?

Sure, they have their butlers put their pants on one leg at a time.

WAS ANDY WARHOL RIGHT THAT EVERYONE WOULD BECOME FAMOUS FOR FIFTEEN MINUTES?

He overestimated.

Warhol lived in a slower time—when film directors often left the same picture on the screen for eight, even nine seconds, when the order of the day was "Ready, aim, fire" instead of the more practical "Ready, fire, aim."

In our faster age, everyone will be famous only long enough for the rest of us to go: Look at him. Who was he, anyway?

WHY DO FAMOUS PEOPLE MARRY OTHER FAMOUS PEOPLE?

Celebrities have a burning need to be understood. They figure only someone else who has gone through the gantlet of celebrity can possibly understand them.

They soon discover, much to their displeasure, that the famous person they marry also wants to be understood.

Since celebrities are good at wanting to be understood

but not at understanding anyone else, they condemn each other never to be understood.

This leads to celebrity divorce, where they finally find someone who understands them: their celebrity spouse's celebrity divorce attorney.

HOW CAN WE RANK THE VALUE OF STARS?

The way we rank everything else—by money: Which movie star has the top box office? Which basketball star gets the biggest salary? Which poet makes $50 a year and which only makes $15?

Let's figure out the nostalgic values of stars. Play along:

When they were auctioned off, which brought in more money?

1. Indiana Jones's bullwhip or Elvis Presley's driver's license?

2. The baseball that rolled through Bill Buckner's legs in game six of the 1986 World Series or the Blues Brothers' dancing suits and sunglasses?

3. James Dean's toy monkey from *Rebel Without a Cause* or Kevin Costner's peace pipe from *Dances With Wolves*?

4. A slice of breakfast toast served to George Harrison (plus a bonus twig from John Lennon's hedge) or Liberace's embossed paper napkins?

ANSWERS

1. Indiana's bullwhip sold for $24,300. Elvis's license for only $7,400.

2. John Belushi and Dan Ackroyd's movie gear went for $12,000. Movie star Charlie Sheen paid $93,500 for the baseball that cursed the Red Sox and immortalized the Mets.

3. Costner's pipe brought in $6,000. James Dean's toy monkey sold for $6,800.

4. Liberace's napkins went for $182. The Beatles' toast and twig sold for $2,000.

From these examples we learn that fame has no inherent value, aside from the nostalgic price tag we hang on the worthless leftovers we sweep up from the toss-offs of fame.

$12,000 for a used suit? $93,500 for a $3 baseball?

I like to think that Charlie Sheen got conned on the Buckner ball, like all those baseballs supposedly autographed by the stars, when they were actually signed in rows by bat boys picking up a little extra in tips by doing a chore that athletes consider stupid.

DO FAMOUS PEOPLE ACTUALLY HAVE A BETTER SEX LIFE?

Not in the physical sense.

But they do have better PR agents, who tell us that they have a better sex life.

The flacks don't promote the fantasy that the famous are privileged to enter an erotic paradise the rest of us will never visit just to stroke celebrity egos.

They are trying not to disappoint us.

They know we want to think that someone must be having the kind of incredible sex life that we don't have but assume we would if we were famous. Otherwise, why would we be so jealous of them?

CELEBRITY DREAMS

As I plunged into the research for this book, famous people began to appear in my dreams every three or four nights. True to the lure of fame, I found myself drawn to these dreams more than other dreams peopled by less celebrated characters. The celebrities were more popular in my own dreams than I was.

Here are a few of those famous dreams:

1. Dustin Hoffman asks to see me. In his vast library, he offers me a job helping him "weave together the strands of the discontinuous."

2. Spencer Tracy comes into my restaurant and orders "the pearl stew."

"Pearl stew?" I ask.

"Yup, then the roast swine."

3. Julia Roberts is driving me to high school to see a baseball game. Looking for a place to park, she pulls into a yellow zone.

"There's a spot up there," I say. "This is yellow."

The spot up ahead is metered. "I don't want to pay to park," Julia says.

"That's okay," I say. "I'll pay for it."

I wake up at that point and instantly realize the significance of the dream: I have more money then Julia Roberts. All right.

4. John Travolta is teaching me how to shoot pool, but we have no cue sticks. We use our noses and fingers instead.

I make a long corner shot and say, "Pretty good, huh?"

John says, "Yeah, but the thing is, you have to get everything else working that well too."

5. Suzanne Somers is doing a TV infomercial, eating dinner while demonstrating a bar-code reading fork that adds up the calories of every bite of food she puts in her mouth.

6. I'm on the set of the TV show *Who Wants to Be a Millionaire*. But I'm not a contestant. I'm there to help my

ancient grandfather, whose dream has been to get on the show.

Regis Philbin thinks my grandfather is too senile to answer questions, especially since he has brought along a cheat sheet, on which he wrote everything he still knows.

Regis asks the first question, but before we can answer, a giant cricket buzzes around our heads. The cricket is so monstrous, people run around the stage screaming.

When the cricket lands on a buzzer, I pick up a carpet sweeper and smash it, which pushes a button and gets the answer right. We win!

But several months later, I realize Regis never sent the money.

7. It's the NBA All-Star game, and I'm sitting on the bench of the West team as the game starts.

The East scores the first few baskets, so coach Phil Jackson calls me over and tells me I'm going in the game.

Then he looks at me funny. Instead of a uniform, I'm wearing a pair of baggy pants with the waistband folded over all around because the pants are too big for me.

"New style?" Coach Jackson asks.

"No belt," I explain.

Is God famous?

We've all heard of him, but no one knows him well enough to sell his secrets to the *National Enquirer*. He has never done a TV talk show, doesn't show up at the right parties.

God is famous the way that diamonds are valuable: Scarcity creates demand.

But as you look up to the vastness of the universe, you have to wonder: Is God famous anywhere but on Earth? If so, does he make personal appearances there?

ARE ALL FAMOUS PEOPLE ECCENTRIC?

To us. Not to their wives.

Which famous man's wife described him this way: "He is not eccentric. He hardly ever mislays things. At least, not more than most men. He knows when it's time for lunch and dinner."

That would be Albert Einstein, who is eccentric because he did not take advantage of his fame.

A fame-optimizing person will order lunch at midnight, dinner every other Thursday. That's the way to build a legend.

DOES FAME MEAN YOU NEVER HAVE TO CLEAN YOUR OWN BATHROOM AGAIN?

Yes, that's the good news. Unfortunately, the people you hire to clean up your mess will poke around in your bathroom for something they can sell to the *National Enquirer*.

Also, there are plenty of poor people who also don't clean up after themselves. I've been in their homes.

Eventually, we'll have a world where no one cleans up anything. It will be dirty, crowded, a mess. Sort of like the one we've got now, but so much more so that we'll look back on this one nostalgically.

WILL BRITNEY SPEARS BECOME AS FAMOUS AS BUDDHA?

More than. Buddha may have found enlightenment, but look at Britney's body.

And she can do her own commercials, whereas Buddha doesn't come into your living room every night; you actually have to seek enlightenment.

The only thing Britney has to worry about: built-in obsolescence. Does anyone really fantasize about Madonna any more?

WHAT WOULD OUR WORLD BE LIKE WITHOUT THE FAMOUS?

We'd all be watching *Not So Entertaining Tonight* and reading *Ordinary People* magazine. *The National Enquirer's* motto would be "Enquiring minds are too polite to ask."

WAS EVERYONE SOMEONE FAMOUS IN A PAST LIFE?

People who claim to be reincarnated were always someone famous in a past life.

What are we to conclude from this pattern? That only famous people get reincarnated.

The meek apparently don't come back. Perhaps they move on to some other plane of existence. Or enjoy a new kind of fame in heaven, where they are celebrated for being among the few to negotiate the moral obstacle course of earthly life.

But if the famous are reincarnated, why do they always come back as ordinary people?

Are they riding a downward spiral of evolutionary incarnations, passing through you and heading toward an eventual life as a cockroach?

IS THE STAR YOU THINK YOU KNOW THE REAL PERSON?

The husband you think you know probably isn't the real person.

But here's what Bob Dylan, the first honest songwriter, had to say about fame and identity: "People think they know me from my songs. But my repertoire of songs is so wide-ranging that you'd have to be a madman to figure out the characteristics of the person who wrote all those songs."

Danny De Vito isn't funny, except when he's hired to play someone who is. Arnie isn't a hero. You wouldn't fall in love with Angelina Jolie offscreen unless her lighting and makeup crew were there to make the magic happen.

IS IT TOUGH BEING FAMOUS?

Can be.

Here's Bob Dylan again: "People ask me if it's hard being me. I answer, 'To a degree, but it's not any more difficult than being George Michael.'"

WHAT WOULD IT BE LIKE IF THEY TREATED THE REST OF US THE WAY THEY TREAT FAMOUS PEOPLE?

If it ever happens, you'll read about it in that supermarket tabloid "Celebrity News for Non-Celebrities." Stories like these:

1. Incredibly average person goes to so-so party

Wallace Baine, who falls on the median more often than most people, went to a party over the weekend, although he almost decided not to go, but then he figured: Why not? Although halfway there, he also figured: Why?

"The pretzels weren't stale," he said, admitting that he had a couple of beers but they didn't do much for him.

That may be Wallace you see in the corner of the photo standing to the side of the food table.

The photo was taken by Peggy Townsend, who spent much of the party debating whether she should switch her major to food-science management and do a study of the potato puff for her thesis.

"Potato puffs?" Peggy was heard to ask Wallace, or perhaps the person standing next to Wallace. "What do you think?"

"I've never been able to really enjoy a potato puff," Baine explained. "You know, because of what happened to Puff the Magic Dragon. Never got over that."

2. Roofers split—maybe

Our Man Halfway Inside reports that Dan Fitch and Travis Semmes, who both work for Sentinel Roofing, have fallen out over proper nail-gun storage techniques and are no longer talking to each other.

A company spokesman denied the allegations, saying Fitch was working on the south side of the roof and Semmes on the north side and that's all it was. Or was it?

3. Nancy and George deny rumors

"We're just friends," Nancy Redwine insisted.

"Actually, we just sort of know each other," George Merilatt explained. "From around."

But our sources say the couple are an item. They were seen lunching together at the fashionable Burger King outside of town.

"We weren't together," insisted Nancy, a part-time nail technician and Web designer. "We were just sitting sort of next to each other."

"You know, the way those little plastic tables they have and those little stool chairs, it's hard to tell which table you're actually sitting at and if the person next to you is with you or just next to you," said George, who is working as a copy-machine technician while studying to be a meter maid or an actor at night.

"I wouldn't say acting," he insisted. "It's just a class in public speaking because, you know."

SHOULD CELEBRITIES BE ALLOWED TO HAVE KIDS?

Only if our supply of completely screwed-up kids is running low.

CAN'T SOME FAMOUS PEOPLE RAISE THEIR KIDS RIGHT?

Stranger things have happened, but not much.

Famous people must decide: How much do they let their fame intrude on their kids' lives?

In the old days, fame was welcomed at the door and given the tour of the house. The kids were either sent away to boarding school or used for cute props in photo ops.

Now security advisers tell the famous to keep their kids under wraps so the children can't be used against them.

Either way, the essentials of a good childhood (love, support, guidance) are almost impossible to achieve under the demands of fame (where the essentials are idolization, manipulation, and exploitation).

SOME CELEBRITIES MUST REALLY LOVE THEIR KIDS

And they show it in ways that would warm the heart of public relations professionals everywhere.

During an interview about a kids' movie, one studio executive told me that he makes sure one of his secretaries attends every soccer game his kid plays in.

In Hollywood that's considered making the extra effort because there's no obvious profit point in the action.

WHY ARE THEY FAMOUS AND WE'RE NOT?

They have a rare dreamy quality that resists mass manufacture. They embody the same sensibility we find in our subconscious longings. They fit into a dream world, not theirs but our own.

We are all famous in our own dreams, where we are the stars because there's no one else there.

Stars fulfill the loss of our dreams. We wake up, but they exist in fame.

Our heroes don't give a damn and we do. They know there's no place like home, while we'd like a good excuse to stay away if we had any other place to go.

They will always have Paris; we never will. Maybe we'll have Trenton, maybe not.

Movie stars always begin to disappoint when they go off-script. See them in person—when they're awake—and you end up singing a sour chorus of "Is That All There Is?"

WHY DO STARS GET DIVORCED MORE THAN MOST PEOPLE GET MARRIED?

Because they can.

Being rich and famous means never having to play with last year's toys.

Picture bandleader Ike Turner (married thirteen times) wheeling his cart around the aisles at the Meet-a-Mart. He bumps into a woman shopping the other way.

"I'm . . . I'm sorry," she says.

"I'm . . . I'm not married today," he replies. "The checker on aisle seven can do the honors. What do you think?"

"Well, I was only here to pick up some soda and mixed nuts."

What exactly is woman #13 thinking when Ike Turner proposes?

Yeah, sounds good. Here's a guy I can turn around. Sure, it didn't work the first twelve times, but he must really mean it this time.

DOES FAME DESTROY BEAUTY?

Unintentionally, and by the second generation. The children of famous men get better looking than their fathers, but the children of beautiful women are uglier than their mothers.

WHY IS THAT?

Because beautiful women marry famous men, and famous men marry beautiful women.

IS IT REALLY LONELY AT THE TOP?

Sure, but it's lonely in the middle and at the bottom too.

At least at the top, there are so many people hovering around that celebrities never get any sense of who they would be if they were left alone to find out, and that's probably just as well.

IS FAME GOOD FOR YOU?

It's like having chocolate cake and champagne for breakfast. Exotic, daring, risqué.

Then for lunch, then for dinner. Then day after day until the very word *cake* makes you cringe with horror and you decide it's no coincidence that the word champagne can be respelled "sham-pain."

DO YOU HAVE TO SELL YOUR SOUL TO BECOME FAMOUS?

No, but clearly it helps, or fewer people would be lining up with for-sale signs pinned to their chests.

Celebrities promote the notion that you have to sell your soul for fame because that's how they did it. Just as misery recruits company, they feel better about selling their soul for glitter if you sell yours too.

DOES FAME MEAN YOU GET TO ABUSE THE LITTLE PEOPLE?

That's one of the main attractions.

Fortunately, many little people will line up to be taken advantage of by anyone even remotely famous.

Take a press junket I attended when I was in the celebrity-story writing business a few years back.

Reporters sat around in a Hollywood hotel, waiting their turn to ask Julia Roberts inane questions and receive inane answers.

The star, who was pushing one of her less-than-great movies, was guided by a flack from table to table for group interviews so that all the reporters could go back to their hometown and write a story that began: "Julia Roberts and I are having coffee in a Hollywood hotel . . ."

Julia didn't drink coffee. But she smoked a lot, and the movie studio assigned someone to rush over, pick up Ms. Roberts's cigarettes and move them to the next table, under the theory that you cannot expect a star of Julia's magnitude to pick up her own cigarettes.

The cigarette chaser took her job as seriously as a ball girl at Forest Lawn.

The timing, the scoop, the glide to the next table, the precise placement and deferential release. The cigarette chaser had proven her talents and reliability to the studio bosses or she would not have been given such an important celebrity job.

WHAT IS THE BEST FIELD IN WHICH TO PURSUE FAME?

Politics?

No, politicians are rare among the famous because they know mathematically how much they're disliked, usually by 49.1 percent of the people, which shows that you don't have to fool all the people all the time; you have to fool only 50.9 percent of them.

Writing?

Excuse me while I put down my computer and laugh.

Writers have one serious drawback to fame: They have to work for it. You try writing three hundred pages; see how much like a celebrity you feel after that.

Rock stars?

Excellent choice, but a caution: You won't want to get on a plane, drive a car, go swimming, or eat too many sandwiches.

As for drugs and booze, rock 'n' roll is one of the few professions where being zonked out of your mind makes absolutely no difference in terms of job performance.

There are two clauses in the contracts of famous rock stars, and you have to sign one or the other:

1. I agree to throw it all away down the neck of a whiskey bottle or the point of a needle so that the supply of beautiful stars who die young will not diminish.

2. If I opt for a long-term deal, I agree to make a ludicrous fool of myself at fifty, prancing awkwardly around the stage trying to remember the words to songs I sang at twenty.

Sports?

You get five years. Then you have to sell insurance and reveal to everyone how stupid you were all along.

Movie stars?

Great choice unless you're an actor.

Film favors lovers over actors. Talent distracts the adoring camera, and fans resent the disruption of their fantasies.

Famous poet?

Just kidding.

Quick, name your favorite poet. Now name #2.

Most people say Robert Frost because he's got a catchy name.

The second-most famous poet in America? Probably Hallmark Cards. If you're going to insist on being a poet, at least change your name to Cassandra Rainyday. Mnemonics are your best strategy.

DOES FAME LEAD TO OVERWEENING PRIDE?

It should, for you will never have to wait tables again.

You will be filled with the profound inner satisfaction that comes from knowing you'll never have to sort through garbage or measure another man's inseam for a suit fitting.

Fame is the ultimate protection from spatulas and welding torches.

HOW CAN YOU TELL THAT YOU'RE ABOUT TO BECOME FAMOUS?

1. Suddenly, people listen to you, especially when you have nothing interesting to say.

2. You have just spent $150,000 on plastic surgery and the doctor wants to put your new breasts in his advertising campaign.

3. Your level of serendipity improves.

For example, you're flipping through the TV channels. But instead of landing on a Burger King commercial, then a *Three's Company* rerun, then a Jack in the Box commercial rerun—you flip from Lexus to golf to BMW.

4. You spot a $20 bill on the street and you think twice about whether it's worth your time to pick it up.

5. When Steven Spielberg calls, you don't assume it's one of your dumb friends playing another stupid gag.

HAVE ALL THE STARS IN HOLLYWOOD SLEPT THEIR WAY TO THE TOP?

Not everyone.

The general guideline: If they look like a Julia or an Uma, they had to.

But if they look like a Roseanne or a Rosie, they weren't asked.

Certainly someone must have made it on talent alone, you say.

Maybe, but they're not statistically significant.

Talent is the tale great PR agents tell.

Of course, to get the great PR agent interested in telling your tale, you probably have to sleep with him.

WHY DO WE WORSHIP FAMOUS PEOPLE?

We have to worship someone. It's a basic human need to think there's someone else not as screwed up as we are.

This accounts for the widespread belief in God.

I was going to call this book *Let's Adore Famous People*. But then I thought: No, that's what we have *People* magazine for.

Not to mention *Vanity Fair,* the *New Yorker, Premiere,* David Letterman, Jay Leno, and the entertainment sections of every major newspaper in the country.

Exactly how much worship do famous people need?

More than they can get, apparently.

Mathematically, the equation goes: their need for fame = our need for them to be famous − our need to destroy our own monsters from time to time × what a cute butt − she's really starting to look her age − how boring it all is.

A NIGHT IN THE LIFE OF A FAMOUS PERSON

Here's one question you never hear a famous person ask: "So what do you want to do tonight?"

That's because famous people have signed on with service outfits like Fame Maintenance Inc. that provide consultation so stars can maximize celebrity payoff in nocturnal activities. Let's peep:

Roger Smartz, consultant: Sir, time to consider your fame-optimizing schedule for tonight.

Hugh E. Gogh, star: I was going to take the night off. What's my rank?

Smartz: Slipping. You're down to 1,075 on the National Fame Register. I don't think we want 1,074 people more famous than you.

Gogh: Is Sylvester?

Smartz: Yes, 1037.

Gogh: Let's get to work.

Smartz: Tonight's scenario calls for a power dinner with full exposure.

Gogh: Shall I dine at Le Lei?

Smartz: That's a negative. The whole French-Hawaiian thing was always suspect. We are recommending Le The today.

Gogh: But the food is terrible.

Smartz: You're not actually going to eat any. Haven't you studied the UCLA Waistline-to-Fame study we sent over? One more inch around the middle and you're out of *Vanity Fair* for a year. Can you afford that?

Gogh: Madonna?

Smartz: 935 and climbing.

Gogh: All right, Le The. What's my move after dinner?

Smartz: The annual Semi-United Way's "Hollywood, Hollywood, Hollywood Cares" fund-raiser for People Who Are Vaguely Suffering. Five minutes max.

Gogh: Charities, I don't know. They can be so needy.

Smartz: Our people are negotiating for wave-and-nod status only.

Gogh: Good, what's next?

Smartz: Then off to no more than 3.7 parties and home by midnight.

Gogh: Alone or with a starlet?

Smartz: That's optional.

Gogh: Should I punch a paparazzi tonight?

Smartz: We recommend a right cross. Your left hook just doesn't have headline impact.

Gogh: Sounds doable. But no more starlets. They want too much.

Smartz: We can find you one less sexually demanding.

Gogh: It's worse than sex. They want contacts. Phone numbers. They want to have their way with my Rolodex.

Smartz: May we suggest our new Insta-A-FFair service? We match you with someone whose fame profile is compatible with your own, and your affair is contractually limited to those activities that will be fame-positive for both of you. You get 24-hour fame protection. It's in the contract.

SO THE FAMOUS ARE ALWAYS THE S'S AND THE REST OF US ARE THE M'S IN THE S&M EQUATION?

No, it works both ways.

Often, famous people are taken advantage of as badly as they assume they can take advantage of others.

Consider the case of Tony Melendez, a thalidomide baby born without arms. As a kid, he taught himself to play the guitar with his feet, which he did on the streets of L.A. to make money for his poor family.

Tony became famous when he played for Pope John Paul II, who kissed the boy on the cheek after he played.

The next morning, Tony woke to three TV news vans parked in front of his house.

Introduction to Fame 101:

"Right after I sang for the pope, there was this big old party someone wanted me to go to," Tony said. "I got there, and they had a fake pope come and kiss me. It didn't seem proper to me."

DO YOU HAVE TO BE GOOD AT SOMETHING TO BE FAMOUS?

Talent often confuses the issue. You can be the greatest French horn player in the world, and you will never be famous because there are no famous French horn players.

But you can be a mediocre TV actor and still be famous. In fact, it's required, the mediocrity, because if you were a great TV actor you'd make everyone else in the show look bad.

THE SIXTEENTH MINUTE OF FAME

Your fifteen minutes of fame are finally over. Then what happens?

In the sixteenth minute: People say, "Didn't you used to be someone?"

In the seventeenth minute: People take their pictures with you, then toss the photo into an old shoe box. When they drag it out a couple of years later, they think you must have been someone they used to work with.

In the eighteenth minute: You have to explain to people who you used to be.

In the nineteenth minute: When you do supermarket openings, the store manager offers to pay your fee in day-old bread.

In the twentieth minute: Your kids have to explain to their friends who you used to be.

In the twenty-first minute: *People* magazine cancels your subscription.

In the twenty-second minute: Your sister has to explain to your mother who you used to be.

In the twenty-third minute: History professors come by and ask, "So what was it like in the old days?"

And you say, "But that was just eight minutes ago."

And they say, "Right, so what was it like in the old days?"

In the twenty-fourth minute: The nostalgia speculators offer to buy your leftover memorabilia. You think maybe you should save them for your own profit, but you have no idea if there will be any.

In the twenty-fifth minute: You mistake your old publicity photos for family shots of your uncle.

WHY DO SO MANY STARS MAKE LOUSY FAMOUS PEOPLE?

Bad training.

Our society gives people extensive training in how to fail, by setting up goals that only .00001 percent of us will ever achieve.

But none of those lucky few who make it have any idea how to handle fame because schools don't teach fame management.

WOULDN'T IT BE FOOLISH TO TEACH KIDS HOW TO BE FAMOUS WHEN SO FEW WILL BE?

We teach math, and few kids become mathematicians.

We teach basketball even though 99.9999 percent of them will not become basketball players.

What we're really teaching them is:

1. Math aversion so they will go into debt as adults and support the giant finance industry for forced debt.

2. How to become basketball consumers so that when the star-and-owner cartel raises ticket prices to $85 for bad seats, they will pay it thinking they're part of the game.

WHY DO FAMOUS PEOPLE HAVE THE WORST MANNERS?

If love means never having to say you're sorry, then fame means never having to say please or thank you.

Being rude is a test of fame. If your rude behavior diminishes your fame quotient, then it demonstrates that you weren't famous enough.

Marlon Brando can snub the Oscars and still land a multi-million-dollar cameo. You probably cannot.

WHAT DO CELEBRITIES REALLY WANT?

1. So much money they don't have to pay any attention to how much they're being cheated by their managers.

2. Enough people telling them how great they are that they forget how much they feel like talentless frauds. They also want a flack defender to point out that anyone who points out that they are talentless frauds is also a talentless fraud.

3. Beautiful people of one sex or the other, or both, who will do whatever they're asked for the chance to see if it's any different bedding famous people.

4. The privilege of complaining that fame is an invasion of privacy, even though they could have their privacy simply by avoiding fame.

DO ALL FAMOUS PEOPLE GET THEIR NEW CLOTHES FROM THE SAME PLACE THE EMPEROR DID?

They are all naked under their Diors, and if they have been working out enough they won't mind proving it.

Haven't you wondered what happened to that smart-mouth kid who pointed out that the emperor's new clothes were a fraud?

The kid wrote a book called *Emperors: Naked or Just Alternatively Clothed?*

Went on the talk show circuit. Was offered fourteen weeks on CNN as emperor-analyst. Got canceled after two weeks when it turned out the only opinion he had was "naked."

Was last seen lying drunk in an alley behind the tailor shop reading William Burroughs's *Naked Lunch*.

HOW HAS FAME CHANGED
OVER THE CENTURIES?

In the past you had to discover an entire continent to become famous. Now you just have to uncover your belly button, and if the right people think you've got a swell one, you're in, baby.

In the past you had to win several major battles to become famous. Now you just have to get on the right talk show and reveal your victory over addiction.

In the past you had to paint the Sistine Chapel. Now a hot rock video will do the trick.

Centuries ago people became famous as great lovers. Where are the Casanovas and Don Juans today? Watching TV like everyone else.

TV has taken the place of sex because it's sexier than sex.

People once craved sexual danger. Now that sex can kill, they can get it safely by watching it on TV. It may not be actually happening to them, but that's a minor difference.

WHY DON'T GAY CELEBRITIES PROCLAIM THAT
THEY'RE GAY AND ADVANCE THE ACCEPTANCE
OF HOMOSEXUALS IN OUR SOCIETY?

There's no profit motive.

Celebrities and their advisers may be gay, but they are also green and don't want to risk box office for an abstract cause.

So gay celebrities stay gray, which leads everyone else into the world of rumors.

Take the case of pop singer Ricky Martin, who when asked if he was gay responded in the guarded fashion of a politician:

"I'm an artist and you can fantasize about me however you want."

Martin's Republicanesque approach (don't say yes or no) was called "a major turning point for pop culture" by the editor of the gay publication the *Advocate*.

Gay celebrities have another option: They can simply come out and say, "Sure, I'm gay. What's it to ya?"

But honesty is looked upon with suspicion in celebrity circles unless everything else fails.

WHAT'S IT LIKE TO MEET A FAMOUS PERSON?

I was walking down the street and there he was, him, Rocky Godd, and I thought: Oh, my god, it's Godd.

And he was, like, so cool. He didn't say anything, but he looked at me like: I know you know and while I don't want everyone else to be bothering me, I would want you to, only you're way too cool to ever do that.

So I said, like, hi, and he was so cool, he said, hi. Just like a regular person, and I said, oh, my god, it's you, and he said, sometimes.

I'll never forget it: sometimes.

Then what happened?

Well, I had to go home to clean my toilet.

And what happened to Rocky Godd?

I don't know. Maybe he had to go home and have someone clean his toilet too. But I'll never forget it.

We rarely meet famous people when they're in the act of doing what made them famous.

In nearly all the encounters we have with the famous, they are doing something ordinary, much like an ordinary person would do it.

You met Jesus at the Laundromat?

Wow. On the one hand, it's Jesus.

On the other, what's he doing at the Laundromat? Odds are it's his laundry. Which puts him in the same rinse cycle as the rest of us.

WHAT'S THE NEW TREND IN FAME?

Niche fame.

You find an area where no one else is famous and claim it. For example, vegetable hurling.

Sorry, already taken.

But there's a lesson to be learned from the Punkin Chunkers of Milton, Delaware.

Bill Thompson, Trey Melson, and John Ellsworth were sitting around in the machine shop one day arguing about how far they could project vegetables.

Being mechanically minded, they set to designing pumpkin-hurling machines (catapults, air cannons, and contraptions too bizarre to describe).

They ran a contest. Went annual. Went international. They hurled a pumpkin through a neighbor's roof when it went off course. Rebuilt the roof. Went back to tinkering with their machines.

They're up to almost a mile now, farther then anyone in history has projected a squash.

Some fifty thousand people attend their contest every year. Wouldn't you? Pumpkin hurling: not the kind of invention that's going to make you much money or an international celebrity (although Bill is pretty much the Brad Pitt of projectile vegetables).

But it will make you unique: niche fame.

IF FAME ISN'T ALL IT'S CRACKED UP TO BE, WHY DO SO MANY PEOPLE WANT TO BECOME FAMOUS?

Because nothing else is what it's cracked up to be either.

You go to work, you're bored. You come home and watch TV and you're still bored.

You attempt one or more hyped activities, but they don't play out as well as they did in the commercials, and then you sprain your ankle.

Then you die, and your friends and family find out that your life can be condensed into one meaningless paragraph in the local paper, in which they probably spell your name wrong.

The only consolation you get is that when the obit writer dies, the next obit writer will condense his life into one meaningless graph and spell his name wrong too.

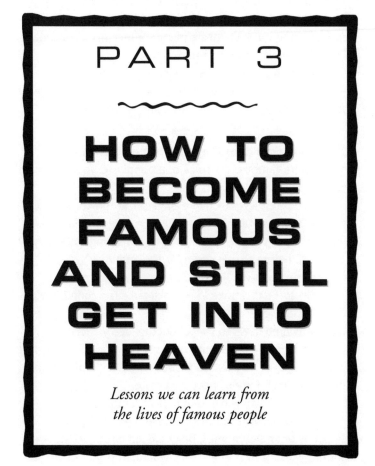

PART 3

HOW TO BECOME FAMOUS AND STILL GET INTO HEAVEN

Lessons we can learn from the lives of famous people

1. Live for your biographer.

Your biographers don't want to be forced to dig up dirt about you. They want it piled up, and high. So give up all pretense of being nice. There are plenty of nice people already.

In baseball nice guys finish last.

In Hollywood they don't even get off the bus.

As Bette Davis, who should know, said: "Until you're known in my profession as a monster, you're not a star."

~~~

2. Break only the rules they say can't be broken.

If you're famous, the rules don't apply to you. Not even the laws of physics.

I once interviewed Charlie Sheen, the movie actor, in a Phoenix hotel suite. He came in from jogging four miles, wiped off with a towel, opened a bottle of spring water and lit a cigarette before sitting down for the interview.

My first question: "How come you run and smoke?"

"I run *so* I can smoke," he explained. "The running wipes out the smoking."

That will be news to cancer doctors everywhere.

Thinking you can do what they say can't be done may not do anything for Charlie's health, but it's the kind of presumption upon which famous people operate.

Are they oblivious because they're famous?

No, they become famous because they're oblivious.

Life is bound by bumps, blocks, dead ends, pitfalls, and a daunting variety of barriers that would stop you or me. But the famous race over them, laughing into the wind and trailing their long scarves.

3. Always change horses in midstream.

The horse you rode in on is probably too tired to get you all the way across.

Before he became a writer and philosopher, Henry David Thoreau went to work for his father, who manufactured pencils. Thoreau conducted experiments and invented a better type of pencil, then quit the business, declaiming, "I would not do again what I have done once."

Steve Martin studied philosophy at California State University at Long Beach and, for a while, considered becoming a philosophy professor instead of an actor-comedian.

Both Thoreau and Martin made the right but opposite decisions by changing horses in midstream.

Thoreau rode out on the horse that Martin rode in on.

~~~

4. Make the ordinary extraordinary.

Pablo Picasso was a great painter who carried that artistic instinct wherever he went.

"When we were in a flea market at Cannes, I saw him buy a pizza, which was served on a paper plate," recalled Picasso's friend Rosamond Bernier. "When he finished the pizza, he took a flower, rubbed the flower into the paper plate and made a drawing with its juices.

"It was a sense of fun and an absolute compulsion to turn one thing into something else."

~~~

5. Invent the details.

Fame finds people who think of the small details that most of us don't realize need thinking about.

Consider Jean Harlow, a movie star who captured

people's imagination in a way that few have since. Picture Julia Roberts and Madonna combined.

Here's an inside look at one of the things Harlow knew that would-be stars didn't know needed to be known.

"You know, Harlow never wore anything, uh, underneath her clothes—like the kids are doing now," actress Joan Blondel said about working with Jean Harlow and James Cagney in the movie *Public Enemy.*

"One day Cagney says, 'How do you hold those things up?' and Harlow said, 'I ice them.'"

~~~

6. Be selective about which mountains you climb.

No one climbs Mount Dinky because it's there. But when you climb an Everest, they'll write down whatever you have to say.

When Katherine Bates made the arduous climb to the top of Pikes Peak in 1893, she was so inspired by the panorama that she wrote the uplifting hymn "America the Beautiful," which we're still singing today down here in the flatlands.

If she had climbed a smaller hill, she might have given us "America? Not Bad."

~~~

7. Get to new ideas first.

Think about new things in new ways because if you don't, others will.

Aerospace magnate Willard Rockwell Jr. understood the constant turnover of creativity as it applies to manufacturing success.

"If we don't obsolete most of our own products ourselves at least every five years," Rockwell said, "our competition will do it for us."

We should obsolete our old thinking the same way. New ideas are coming anyway. If they don't come to us, they will come to the people we'd rather they didn't.

～～～

8. No more Mr. Nice Star.

Shuck the modesty. It wasn't convincing anyone anyway.

Truman Capote may not have been the greatest writer the world has ever known, but you couldn't tell him that.

"I've known all my life I could take a bunch of words and throw them up in the air and they would come down just right," he proclaimed. "I'm a semantic Paganini."

Capote was better known for his proclamations than his writing. They don't invite a lot of good writers onto TV talk shows. But they do invite their share of funny little men in white suits with affected mannerisms and the wit to convince people that this must be what a Paganini of words is like.

～～～

9. Don't wear shorts.

Even if you think you can get away with it, you can't.

Fashion designer Rudi Gernreich: "A little pair of shorts is more difficult to wear than a skirt. A skirt may hide part of the behind that may not be perfect, whereas in a pair of shorts you can see the outline and the curve easily. And if it's not really pretty, you're kind of in trouble."

What does this petty advice have to do with fame?

It's a petty world where people are always evaluating your butt and everything else you do.

You want to make a good impression, especially when your back is turned.

10. Make your gestures dramatic.

You can hardly ever go over the top in this world. Subtlety is what gets missed on Saturday night.

Make your statements dramatic and preferably ruinous. People want that vicarious thrill of watching you take your life in your hands.

At a New York fair in 1854, an unknown, in-debt engineer stood on a platform high above a crowd and cut the ropes that held the platform aloft. Instead of plunging to its destruction, the platform held, and Elisha Otis became famous. He had invented not the elevator but the safety elevator.

Another engineer, whose name we don't remember, invented the elevator. Otis, whose name remains legend, invented the dramatic elevator gesture.

Without his work, Manhattanites would now be complaining about three-story low-rises blocking their view of the sky as they reclined on their lawn chairs.

11. Be incredibly generous when you don't have to be.

I've had five people tell me stories about actor Bill Murray, and they're all about how much money he spreads around as tips.

Murray, they say, keeps a fold of hundreds in his pocket and hands them out for the smallest niceties.

Why? He can afford it, obviously. So can all the other rich and famous, but they don't because they don't have to. He does because he can. Don't you like him better already?

12. Think about your underwear in a new way.

Would Tom Cruise have broken out of the ranks of good-looking young actors who made indifferent films if he hadn't performed that one great dancing underwear scene in *Risky Business*?

The undershorts made him a superstar.

Some eighteen years after that otherwise forgettable movie made Cruise famous, an extroverted high school senior appeared on campus for Halloween dressed in a button-down shirt and his undershorts. He was doing Tom Cruise, and everyone knew who he was doing and they thought it was great, especially the teachers. He's a campus legend now, got that touch of fame early and is moving on.

How are you doing in your underwear?

Clark Gable rocked the entire inside-clothes industry by not wearing his undershirt in *It Happened One Night*. At that time, everyone else wore undershirts. He didn't. That made him news.

Remember Marilyn Monroe's underpants flashing in the billowing dress scene from *The Seven Year Itch*? That scene is still being imitated today in an age when the average Britney shows more skin in soda commercials than Marilyn ever did this side of a pinup calendar.

The wildly popular *Bridget Jones's Diary* is largely the story of a woman and her underwear.

Come up with some new twist underneath and your fame is practically ensured.

13. Don't hold anything back.

You can't save fame the way you hoard money.

On TV when they say live life to the fullest, they mean drink a lot, act like a jerk, and buy everything we have to sell.

But living life to the fullest means using whatever you've got to do things you didn't think you could do, or other people didn't think you could do.

North Carolina State basketball coach Jim Valvano had his perspectives right when he said: "That's what I want— not the money but the whole thing: the energy, the life, and the love for life. I want it all spent."

~~~

14. Don't work too hard.

Movie star Ingrid Bergman explained the secret of romancing the camera: "Keep it simple. Make a blank face and the music and the story will fill it in."

~~~

15. Try farming.

The hard life will motivate you to get off the farm and into the fame business as a way of not having to pull weeds any more.

Worked in the fifth century for Attila the Hun, who found farming so appalling that he pushed his Huns into constant warfare, always charging off to conquer the next people down the line so he wouldn't have to do something with all that land he had already conquered.

That way he managed to conquer nearly the entire known world, and he earned the title of the Scourge of God, which sounds like someone who would do well in the WWF.

~~~

16. Step to the front of the line.

But only when the credit is being handed out.

If you can be a genius, good, work that angle. But genius is rare and as often resented as rewarded.

If you can't be a genius by achievement, you'll have to take the credit for it.

Consider Christopher Columbus. He never would have discovered the New World if it wasn't for someone no one has heard of.

Columbus and his three ships would have sailed right past America if he had stayed on their original course.

But Martin Alonso Pinzón, who piloted the *Pinta*, finally convinced Columbus to change course, and that's how they discovered midtown Manhattan, Hollywood, and your hometown, for which Pinzón got no credit at all.

You ever been to the District of Pinzón?

~~~

17. Trust your enemies.

They will do more to build your legend then your friends will ever do for you.

Famed football coach Bear Bryant turned the University of Alabama into a national powerhouse by intimidating rivals.

As one coach he defeated every year said of Bryant, "He can take his'n and beat your'n, and then take your'n and beat his'n."

Bryant disclaimed his coaching as the key ingredient in the Crimson Tide's legendary success. He promoted this strategy: "Don't get yourself a bunch of tricky plays. Get yourself a bunch of tricky players."

In this way Bryant built his legend as an unbeatable coach, not by convincing his friends or even his team but by convincing rival coaches that they couldn't prepare for Alabama because you can't predict, and even he didn't know, what those tricky players would do next.

18. Don't shine, flash.

Newspaper mogul William Randolph Hearst spent several fortunes to build and decorate the absurdly gaudy Hearst Castle on the central California coast, the kind of home where they should have left the price tag on everything since its only conceivable purpose was to impress the guests.

When playwright George Bernard Shaw visited the Hearst estate at San Simeon, he said, "This is probably the way God would have done it if He had had the money."

God didn't. Hearst did. He spent a fortune to show people that he could afford to throw away that much money.

Decades after his death, few people remember Hearst's dubious work as a newspaper publisher. Millions remember the castle as the kind of grand palace they'd never be invited to.

19. Pump up your charisma.

You can develop charisma muscles the same way you flatten your abs.

Charisma is a key to fame because it makes people listen to whatever you say, even if it's the same thing they ignore when other people say it.

If you have charisma, people will want to spend time with you even if you're cleaning fish.

With charisma, people will think they like you even when they don't know you.

To develop your charisma, be more playful. Don't go in straight lines. Zigzag when there's no point to it. Don't stand in lines. Never plod. Leave more energy behind than you found when you arrived.

Movie star Clark Gable build a career upon charisma

alone, and he could explain it: "The only reason they come to see me is that I know life is great," he said, "and they know I know it."

~~~

20. Happiness first, money second.

While money can't buy happiness, it's possible that happiness may buy money.

Find something you're driven to do by inner compulsion, and the money may follow.

Broadway producer Sol Hurok offered this perspective on the theater: "If I would be in this business for business, I wouldn't be in this business."

Despite his frequent frustrations with the theater, he made several fortunes from it.

If you love what you are compelled to do, then you may attract people who want a touch of that happiness, and they will bring the money with them.

~~~

21. Go your own way, even when you're walking down their road.

Group fame is like watered-down coffee. It's better than nothing, but you drink it only if there's nothing else available.

"I was always an independent," movie mogul Samuel Goldwyn said, "even when I had partners."

~~~

22. Be difficult.

Contrariness is a sign of intelligence and a prerequisite to success.

Consider what Winston Churchill's chief of staff said about

working with England's great wartime leader: "I shall always look back on the years I worked with him as some of the most difficult and trying ones in my life.

"For all that, I thank God that I was given the opportunity of working alongside of such a man and of having my eyes opened to the fact that occasionally such supermen exist on this earth."

Everyone remembers the superman and forgives him his orneriness, the way they don't forgive us our common churlishness. But who remembers the chief of staff?

23. Get extraordinarily lucky.

Andy Devine was walking down the street wearing a football jersey when he passed a casting director who happened to be making a football movie. Devine was hired on the spot, and that's how he became a Hollywood actor.

Fame by luck is the sweetest fame of all because you don't have to work for it and you probably don't deserve it.

No one will resent you for succeeding on pure dumb luck. Instead, they'll identify with you. You could be them, except for the luck part, of course, and the succeeding part.

24. Do it before you think about it.

Fame is not an intellectual pursuit. Thinking makes Hamlets of us all. Acting makes Mel Gibsons.

No, probably not, is the inevitable conclusion of most consideration, while fame is often the result of going for something when you're not quite sure of where you're going.

Historian and author Daniel Boorstin, one of our elite thinkers, understood that cognition is often the effect, not the cause.

"I write to discover what I think," he said.

25. Be eccentric but profitable.

Famous people are eccentric because they can afford to be. The residents of Bedlam are eccentric because they got caught.

With enough money, people will say: He may be crazy, but he's not stupid.

Comic legend Red Skelton understood why his daffiness succeeded. "I have a sixth sense, but not the other five. If I wasn't making money, they'd put me away."

~~~

26. Keep moving forward relentlessly.

As the great author Goethe countered when someone offered a toast to memory, "One is not allowed to pine for the past. Everything significant that has happened is incorporated into oneself and with this one grows."

Goethe was eighty years old when he made that brave assertion.

~~~

27. Be distinctively bad.

If you were a voice coach, you probably would have suggested that Johnny Cash and Bob Dylan consider the advantages of careers in welding or certified accounting. You would not have predicted they would become two of the most popular and enduring singers of their generations.

Yet, we can pick out their voices anywhere, whereas hundreds of singers with vastly superior voices are singing away in your local shower.

Humphrey Bogart, Katharine Hepburn, Meryl Streep, Robert De Niro—not your classic Hollywood beauties. But distinctive. Memorable faces, romantic in their own way, and that's the key: They found their own way.

28. To thine own self be false.

If you can fool yourself, you can fool other people too.

Few people have what it takes to be famous on talent alone. They need to develop the style of a famous person, to put on the cloak of fame the way a model puts on that pouty, pouty face.

What in the world does she have to be pouty about? Everyone thinks she's beautiful and she's getting paid a fortune to stand around and let them think that.

Actor Daniel Day-Lewis knew that before actors can fool other people they must fool themselves.

"I have a highly developed capacity for self-delusion," Day-Lewis said. "So it's no problem for me to believe I'm somebody else."

~~~~

29. Develop a taste for masochism.

If you don't love rejection and abuse, you will take no for an answer, which is how they thin the herd.

If you are an actor and go to, say, five auditions a day, you can be rejected 1,500 times a year, unless you take time off on Sundays for weeping.

Writer Elizabeth Bishop observed a story that was returned by a magazine with "two rejection slips enclosed, which seems unnecessarily cruel."

~~~~

30. Go nuts on offense, soft on defense.

When the great Genghis Khan and his Mongols were conquering much of the world in the thirteenth century, the so-called barbarian proved how civilized he was at psychological warfare.

Khan was so merciless to any enemy he defeated on the battlefield that many armies simply ran at the sight of his horde, saving the Mongols from a fight they might or might not have won.

Once he had taken control of a new territory, Khan changed tactics. Much to the surprise of the defeated, he often didn't slaughter them all (which was the style among conquerors back then, and pretty much now too).

Instead, Khan provided food, security, and religious freedom to the conquered people, who often were better off under the conqueror than when they had been ruled by their own leaders.

~~~

31. Listen to Baudelaire, Emerson, and Churchill.

French poet Charles Baudelaire: "One must astonish the bourgeois."

They need all the astonishment they can get, and they're not going to get that from TV.

Winston Churchill: "No one can guarantee success in war, but only deserve it."

No one can guarantee fame; only you can guarantee the effort.

Ralph Waldo Emerson: "Always do what you are afraid to do."

People are drawn to courage because they need it as much as you do.

Or listen to Flaubert, Freud, and Hugo.

Gustave Flaubert: "You can calculate the worth of a man by the number of his enemies and the importance of a work of art by the harm that is spoken of it."

Don't take your critics to heart, capitalize on their criticisms.

Sigmund Freud: "We are so made that we can only derive intense enjoyment from a contrast and only very little from a state of things."

The more you struggle for fame, the more intense will be your victory.

Which brings us to Victor Hugo and his clarion call: "If suffer we must, let's suffer on the heights."

~~~

32. If all else fails, here's solace:

Lawyer and diplomat Dwight Morrow pointed out that "the world is divided into people who do things and people who get the credit. Try, if you can, to belong to the first class. There's far less competition."